2 βX

7/04

Puritan,
Paranoid, Remissive

By the same author

The Break-Out from the Crystal Palace (1974)

Puritan, Paranoid, Remissive

A Sociology of Modern Culture

John Carroll

Department of Sociology
La Trobe University

Routledge & Kegan Paul
London, Henley and Boston

First published in 1977
by Routledge & Kegan Paul Ltd
39 Store Street,
London WC1E 7DD,
Broadway House,
Newtown Road,
Henley-on-Thames,
Oxon RG9 1EN and
9 Park Street,
Boston, Mass, 02108, USA
Photoset in 11 on 12 Garamond
by Kelly and Wright, Bradford-on-Avon, Wiltshire
and printed in Great Britain by
Lowe & Brydone Ltd

British Library Cataloguing in Publication Data

Carroll, John, b.1944
Puritan, paranoid, remissive.
1. Puritans 2. Religion and sociology
I. Title
309.1'181'2   BL60   77-30015

ISBN 0 7100 8622 9

for Charlotte Zinn von Zinnenburg

Contents

Preface

Social understanding in a time of major cultural transition, when inherited modes of action and representation are tangled up in a complex *mêlée* with new strivings whose shape has not yet emerged, depends on having a clear view of what the old culture signified, how its mechanisms of restraint and release operated, which individual and social functions it fulfilled, and impeded, and ultimately how resistant psychologically it might prove to being shaken off. This is the case with Puritanism now, at a time in the West when it retains some grip over both individual character and collective ideology, a grip which is being shifted and loosened in ways that will determine the course of future possibility. Through a scrutiny of the Puritan ideal and of its decline, of some of its leading manifestations and their internal contradictions, we should gain some sense of what we have inherited, of what we are in the process of losing, and in what ways we may be alternately better and worse off for that loss.

This is an essay in the sociology of contemporary Western culture. It will study the emergence of a new culture, termed 'remissive', from the ruins of the old Puritan order, by taking as *leitmotif* the historical phenomenon of the decline of individual authority. The analysis is pinned to three ideal-types, representing the significant progressive moments in that decline. The pure form of individual authority is identified with the psychological paradigm of the 'Puritan character'. Its final eclipse is represented in the paradigm of 'remissive-hedonist man', and the culture that he inhabits. An intermediary character, the paranoid, features both historically and psychologically in the transition from Puritan to remissive modes of conduct.

A society marshals many psychological types. My argument is that the West is moving from a time when the Puritan type was dominant, in its influence over key social, economic and cultural patterns, to a time when paranoid and remissive types have risen to demote the Puritan into relative obscurity.

Every sociology depends on a series of compromise simplifications. This essay brackets out all but three psychological types. Its other serious mannerism, which ought to be mentioned lest the reader be distracted, is its method of argument. I argue by implication, making associations which vary widely in genus, drawing on examples which may often seem too heterogeneous to bear relation to each other. If a thesis gains shape it does so from the thicket of multiple illustration. This method suffers peculiarly acutely from the problem of all methods, that it depends on relating explicitly the weight of each example and the collective weight of all the examples to the theory. But such explicitness can be achieved only by the art of plausible suggestion, that is, if the work is not to be deafened by hundreds of pages of tuning.

The attention of the essay is restricted to the advanced industrial nations of the West this century. Material is drawn largely from the Anglo-Saxon world, and in particular from the USA. I have not attempted to address the case of the development of capitalism in France, and the question of how decisive a role was played by the Huguenots and by those surrogate Calvinists, the Jansenists. The argument, moreover, does not attempt to encompass all of society, but focuses on that segment conventionally referred to as the upper middle class, or the bourgeoisie, that is on that segment characterized by relative material affluence, high levels of education and occupations that range from the professions to management and administration. In modern industrial societies this class very nearly has a monopoly control of power and taste. Trade unions constitute the only significant power nexus outside its domain, and even their cultural independence is in doubt. With aristocracies either marginal or extinct, and with the remnants of what once might have been a distinctive working-class culture serving at best as a leisure-time affectation, upper-middle-class command of value and fashion is virtually uncontested. In short, this essay concerns itself with the social class in the West whose influence over patterns of behaviour and belief now rules with unprecedented thoroughness an empire of unprecedented reach.

The essay is divided into two parts. The first is the argument proper, written into six chapters that deal in turn with the three ideal-types, the nature of authority in modern Western society, the role of paranoid behaviour in the present cultural transition, and, finally, the viability of the emerging remissive culture.

The second part comprises six footnote chapters, in which various methodological problems that arise during the argument are looked at in some detail. This part plays something of the role of a maintenance department in a trans-continental trucking corporation.

I am deeply grateful to Sandra Lauderdale for many testing comments, and to Ronald Bush for scrupulous stylistic criticism.

J.C.

part 1

The Argument

1

The Puritan

The label 'Puritan' has been applied casually to historical groups, to styles of family and social life, and to traditions of theology, morality and political ideology that flowered in England and New England during the seventeenth century. And indeed there was no homogeneous entity, seventeenth-century Puritanism. But, it is possible to isolate a series of themes, with theological origins, that gained a psychological weight and coherency, and read them as central to many of the areas of religious, social and political movement summed up as 'Puritan'. Taken together these themes constitute a Puritan character, a psychological ideal-type. In constructing this type I have drawn on a range of historical material, the more important of which is listed in the bibliography. My ambition here is not to make any contribution to seventeenth-century history, but to give an account of that history without grotesque simplifications, and then to use it for my own purposes.

It should be recognized from the outset that the individual qualities or virtues that constitute Puritanism's defining personality are not unique to it alone. It shares traits, for example, with Judaism, with ancient Stoicism, with the teachings of Saint Augustine, with the monastic tradition and with Manichaeism. Moreover, it can be loosely conceived of as an admixture of medieval asceticism and Renaissance individualism. Only the whole, as a coherent entity, is unique.

Five distinct clusters of symbol and belief, drawing on Calvinist theology, govern the Puritan character.

1 The doctrine of election, that some men are chosen, and others are not, for grace or salvation. But even those who might consider themselves chosen were hounded by doubt. Election was never assured; a man might be deceived about himself; then again he might lose his grace. The Puritans lived as if sin was binding. Many

believed that sin is never expelled, grace is given to resist it. Thus
guilt, manifest in part as doubt-fed anxiety, is inescapable. They
believed that a man illustrates his election - or the lack of it - by his
conduct. For Puritans, the highest art was the art of living.

2 The quality of a man's life, its moral tone, is a private matter
between his conscience and his God. Thus, contrary to traditional
belief, a man is moral not necessarily by reason of what he
contributes towards the well-being of his fellow citizens, nor is
morality a matter for communal assessment. This doctrine brought
with it a series of new emphases, on constant introspection, on
self-scrutiny, on the individual being totally honest about himself,
his acts and their motives - indeed acts were to be judged in terms of
their motives. It fostered an intense rationality about theological
and psychological matters. Finally, by degrading the normative
power of community, it provoked the individual to live more in
solitude, alone with himself; it made him hesitant both to express
emotion publicly and to form casual intimacies. It imposed a heavy
psychological burden without providing any easy consolations; it
insisted that life be harsh and tempering. The elect could never be
self-satisfied nor supercilious; theirs was a constant burden, not to
be taken on lightly.

3 The doctrine of election, which holds that sin is binding,
implies that there can be no forgiveness. Penance, not penitence, is
all that is available to the Puritan as a means for assuaging his guilt.
The *Westminster Confession*, prepared by the Assembly of Divines
which first met in 1643, probably the most important single Puritan
document, does allow for repentence and eternal salvation.
However, it stresses the infinite distance separating pitiful man
from his God, man's original sin through Adam, and holds that
man cannot choose to repent: repentance comes like salvation as a
gift of God. The demands the *Confession* placed upon the elect
meant they would live as if they were fallen, hoping through
diligence and sobriety to attain salvation in some indeterminate
future. There is no sense of the elect as children of paradise, moving
with the gaiety of angels; rather they lived a constant, vigilant,
working penance. In real, psychological terms, their guilt was never
expiated, their salvation never assured: there was no effective
repentance.

4 A man illustrates that he is chosen through his works: in
particular he finds his vocation or calling in life. Class was not a

barrier to calling: indeed Puritanism undermined the traditional social hierarchy, which had decreed that human worth and godliness was a function of the prestige of the station into which a man is born. Puritanism extended religion beyond the confines of the church, making it this-worldly and tying the individual through his vocation to his environing society. It thus loaded the Puritan with another tension, in that he committed himself to demonstrating his election publicly, in his works, thereby baring himself to communal approbation. Moreover, the Puritan, already burdened by an exacting conscience, sought another dimension of public recognition, support and sanction: he felt driven to publicize his spiritual experience of redemption. During the seventeenth century there was a flood of exhortatory spiritual diaries. In consequence, the family, the social institution most intermediate between private and public, was endowed with a new social (in particular, religious and educational) dignity and authority.

5 Vocation was conceived as a passion, an enduring and inexorably compelling part of an individual's emotional life, contrasting with rhythms of being characterized by ephemeral, impulsive feelings, by infatuations. Vocation as passion, and as the emblem of election, demands to be pursued with relentless discipline, and with an ultimate degree of technical perfection. Vocation is often, in the later terms of Freud, the unabating sublimation of the guilt provoked by a particular sin, or a particular disposition of character, and manifests itself as sustained penitential work.

A subtler strain in Puritanism, and in particular in Puritan literature, recognizing original sin, pursued the implications of it being of man's nature to be hounded by guilt. In the beginning for the individual there was guilt. He did not fall from grace primarily because of a particular act of his own. He was a sinner from birth, and what his personal character determined was not whether he would sin, but the specific ways in which he would express his satanic impulses. The particular acts in his life were not important, they had no innovative function: they were merely the devices by which he made his predetermined nature explicit. Thus his virtue was to be measured by how he coped with his fallen state.

For the Puritan nothing is forgotten: a man's acts articulate his being, which is a coherent entity. He can never say in retrospect,

'That was not me', or 'I was outside myself'. The hero is judged by what Milton referred to as God's representative in man, conscience, a guardian with an infallible memory. Moreover, a theology which does not recognize mistake or aberration has no concept of absolution or remission. Nathaniel Hawthorne wrote that the breaches that guilt makes into the human soul are never repaired. Bunyan's characteristically mercenary metaphor was of a man getting into debt, being able by virtuous acts to pay off the interest, but never the principal.

Max Weber, in his work on the Protestant Ethic, stressed that one goal of Puritan asceticism was for the individual to be able to lead an alert, intelligent life. This goal was symptomatic of a need for pervasive control. Urgent was the task of circumscribing spontaneous, impulsive enjoyment, curbing licentiousness. Even friendship, a Puritan innovation and ideal, was achieved rarely and reticently, a creation of the spirit as much as the heart: contacts with the outside world were established under strict control. The pervasive purity *leitmotif* seems to reveal a fear of being stained, an anticipatory shame that inner secrets might be publicly betrayed. The fall had the metaphoric significance of a descent from pure, private spirit to a nether-world governed alternately by public routine, or 'deadness of heart', and epidemics of sensuality. But we should not forget that the Puritan's great achievement in marriage, an institution to which he gave a new centrality and dignity, was the fusion of sensual and spiritual love. Moreover, seventeenth-century Puritans enjoyed their cakes and ale.

Puritanism became a uniquely effective social force by subordinating public interest to the individual's pursuit of salvation. The practical and the spiritual were fused in this-worldly activity. But the fusion was not a simple one of exclusion. There was at the same time a competing emphasis: the public course of a man's life was seen as being complemented by a private, inner destiny, separate and yet dependent. Indeed, many of the levels at which the Puritan psyche manifests itself are best viewed in terms of a clear division between the domains of private and public, while not forgetting that the domains are inextricably related. (This split between public and private will be clarified in the footnote chapter on Hawthorne's *The Scarlet Letter*. Some attention will also be paid there to that paradoxical Puritan logic that casts guilt and passion as mutually supporting and infusing, and to the role of vocation.)

While Puritan theology worked in the direction of emancipating the individual from the bonds of traditional medieval society, it also stressed man's general responsibility for what happens on earth and, specifically, his need to form under covenant a community with his fellow men. Puritans, and notably the settlers of New England, built communities tightly knit by their common religious and social purpose. Strict private forms were matched by strict public ones. Respect for intellectual prowess was integrated with a respect for this-worldly pragmatism to make the vocations both of minister and magistrate of supreme importance.

The Puritan character can be viewed as a structure whose most important function is to protect itself from despoliation. An exhortatory ideal of purity complements a striving for excellence. Anything short of perfection smirches: the search for divine truth renders other goals trivial and degrading. The Puritan disdains the public world of society and its day-to-day concerns, governed by man's compromises and imperfections, except in that he can succeed in creating within it projects framed by his own ethical demands, directed by his own salvation. It was the Puritan's notion of a 'calling' which ensured both that his spiritual endeavours would take the non-monastic form of work within the community, and that they would be judged according to strict standards of excellence. His duty was to approach his vocation in a fashion that would make of it something exemplary, worthy of an instrument of God. The early Protestant divines of sixteenth-century England emphasized the notion of calling to give work a new dignity, portraying it as creative and enjoyable, and leaving behind the traditional Catholic view of work as penal.

Aspiration towards perfection, coupled with the complementary drive for emotional control, for insulation against pathos, produced the frigidity of character which has so often been attributed to the Puritan. The Puritan took on a mission that was self-absorbed and precluded much interest in, or sympathy for, other human beings and their weaknesses. His notable talent for analysis, whether it be economic, philosophical, theological or finally psychological, could flourish precisely because of his emotional detachment; he preferred at all costs to mediate the world through mind. Where he did look beyond himself it was to the elect, or the élite, as models of conduct and spiritual bearing. These attitudes ran directly contrary to Catholicism's concern for pathos (emotion) rather than ethos (character), its catering for the mass, for the sentimental needs of the common man. Puritanism, taking the Calvinist doctrine of election in its most severe form, concerned itself exclusively with those who had the individual resources to make of their lives something distinguished. It was nowhere as merciless as in its attitude towards failure.

What was compelling about the Puritan at his best was his spiritual intensity. The individual as phenomenon reached a highpoint in Puritan culture: he projected the image of a being under the harness of ascetic control, constantly strained by his scourging intellect, yet, within the compass of this introverted concentration, possessing untold depths. His essential characteristic was *in-tensity*, inner tension, which also gave him access of insight into the core of human passions. If his vices were to be listed they would not include superficiality; his fear was never of being empty or boring. When Puritan character failed its traits were pedantic earnestness, strident moralizing, hysteria, icy detachment, or a melancholia brought on by the crushing burden of conscience. When Puritanism taken as a social force degenerated, it produced either Victorian hypocrisy and prudishness, or an obsessive concern with economic efficiency and maximization engineering. Weber wrote of the modern Protestants: 'specialists without spirit, sensualists without heart'. But the early Protestants had been men of *passion*.

The notion of election, and the derivative belief that salvation is a private matter between the individual and his conscience, the scrupulous demands for purity and perfection, generated a sense of individual responsibility that bared every human act to moral scrutiny. The qualities of intensity, inwardness and self-control combined with the inability either to forgive or to repent, and formed a character marked by its independence, its capacity to stand alone, its command both over its inner self and its public performance of vocation. This character's stature was one of authority. It was not to be lightly swayed, not to be easily crushed.

Believing that each man should accept full authorship of his acts, the Puritan lived as if he had full control over the configuration of his behaviour, as if he should be praised for its virtue and blamed for its vice. But at the same time, he accepted that his virtue was fated, thus that there could be neither free-will nor moral dignity. In fact there is a series of contradictions within the Puritan persona, all amplifying the root absurdity that the individual spent his life atoning for his guilt under the hopeful illusion that redemption was possible, that truth would finally reveal itself. (Sustained work, however the Puritan rationalized it as a means for illustrating his divine predestination, is, psychologically, the product of a drive for atonement.) At the same time the Puritan's knowledge, reinforced by his theology, told him that he was irretrievably fallen, that there was neither absolution nor truth.

When such a character manifested himself publicly, choosing an arena like the political in which to dispel some of his demons, his involvement was marked by deep seriousness, cautious evaluation, and yet, in spite of scrupulous rationality, the passion to choose and to act. The reports of Max Weber, as teacher, social commentator and political participant, illustrate the canopy of charismatic authority under which the Puritan can apply his techniques of ethically reflected rationality to social problems. (They also illustrate the vulnerability of that character to extra tension, the impotence to which Weber was reduced for the five years during which he found himself unable to work.) Milton presents himself as the finest spokesman for this. His portrait of Samson's father's reaction to his son's death remains the final word on Puritanism's cumulative intensity of passionate restraint, of fierce equanimity, of sheer clarity in the face of chaos and cruel fatality:

> Nothing is here for tears, nothing to wail
> Or knock the breast, no weakness, no contempt,
> Dispraise, or blame, nothing but well and fair,
> And what may quiet us in a death so noble.

The Puritan had a strong sense of this-worldly reality. He did not spend energy wishing that his character were different, hoping that he might change himself. His theology told him that his disposition was given and he should do the best he could with what he had; his sense of responsibility was over what he was, over his own character; his introspection was directed at knowing, but not changing, that character; his vocation was chosen according to what suited him personally. The Puritan viewed society from a similar perspective. He sought to make the best of what was there. Even in the extreme case of his finding his own society so corrupt that he chose to leave, he did so in order to set to the practical tasks of founding a viable community elsewhere.

In his own writing Weber showed the manner in which the Protestant and in particular the Calvinist ethic had generative affinities with the type of individual temperament necessary for the development of modern Western social institutions. The asceticism at the root of Calvinism combined with the doctrine of election and its derivative notions of personal calling and responsibility to reinforce and legitimate the new type of rational conduct prerequisite for the evolution of complex economic structures. Christopher Hill has, moreover, in his recent work on seventeenth-century England, argued for links between Cromwell's period of Puritan government and the acceleration of modern science. At another level, Puritanism, in its questioning of existing hierarchy and authority, in its denial of absolution or that there is any final court of appeal, served to increase a general anxiety about salvation and to introduce fear that there might be an arbitrariness about the order of things. It thus added to the anxious rootlessness prevalent in a seventeenth-century Britain which was experiencing rapid political and social change. This rootlessness proved indispensable to the rise of the bourgeois-competitive social model. In Hill's formulation, it undermined the obstacles to capitalism.

In short, Puritanism must be considered one of the shaping forces in the growth of Western industrialized civilization, and perhaps in the expansion of its core of intellectual media, science and technology. Its importance lies in the way it formed the key traits of the psychological character-type who engineered this history. However, I am in this analysis assuming much more. I take the Puritan as the general ideal-type of the culture that attained its maturity in Europe before the First World War. The Puritan metaphor requires some further explanation when applied outside the boundaries of specifically economic development. This essay takes as its foundations the psychological roots of culture. Here it recognizes Nietzsche's stress, in his genealogy of morals, on asceticism as the central thread in European history, and Freud's emphasis on instinctual renunciation as the psychological dynamic for the sublimation that creates culture. Puritanism was the dominant post-Renaissance form in which European asceticism found expression. This expression demonstrated unique affinities with subsequent institutional and cultural development. Puritanism thus selects itself as the organizing symbolic for typifying the motivational foundations of our waning culture.

Nevertheless, my thesis requires a leap of faith at this point. I have used seventeenth-century historical material to construct my ideal-type. I now move to the end of the nineteenth century, from where the essay proper takes its departure, and assert the meaningfulness of employing the Puritan psychological type as the dominant cultural paradigm of the time. This view is defended implicitly in the essay proper through comparative examination of cultural change in the twentieth century. But I have bypassed the formidable task of following the history of the Puritan type through the intermediary two centuries, a task whose completion would strengthen the argument.

Finally, to state my method another way. Behind the manifold process which we from our many perspectives call history, individual character paradigms crystallize and dissolve. Our task then is, like a still-photographer, to make detailed portraits of key moments, which, when viewed together, will bring out the lines of significant change. My use of the ideal character as paradigm is not intended as a mystical notion, some god pulling the strings of history; it is the human nexus, abstracted and simplified, which culture and society at the moment under scrutiny support. What is more, culture and society are available to be read in their paradigm individual, not as its effects, as epiphenomena, but as its *alter ego*, or to combine awkwardly two other lanky metaphors, as both its gene pool and its diffracted image. The tasks of genetics and spectroscopy undertaken here are consequently not aimed at laying bare first causes or final effects, but at interpreting the manner and shape of life as individuals are able to live it during the considered interval on the cultural historical continuum. For individuals do have a greater facticity, or circumscribed coherence, than other entities to which social scientists orient themselves; they are bound by birth and death, and some sort of homeostatic process governs their being, so that there is explicit foundation to talk of a psychic logic, for instance one of control and release, with its assumption of 'organism' - that to influence one segment is to influence the whole. Above all, it is as such individuals that we experience life.

2

The Paranoid

The original Greek sense of 'paranoia' was distraction, the mind beside itself, dislocated; the spirit out of joint. In this essay the term is used in its more specific modern sense of a state of delusion. An individual is deemed paranoid who misreads his reality as persecuting or aggrandizing, who lives by exaggerated suspicions and fears, or by exaggerated hopes. The term is not employed here in its extreme or limiting sense of psychotic paranoia; nor has there been any attempt to incorporate the technical literature of the psychiatric clinic, although parallels between cases of psychotics and those discussed here are marked.

In the paranoid we find a dichotomization of the private and the public similar to the Puritan's, but with reversed focus. The paranoid has lost confidence in private authority. He lives in fear of domination or threat from his environment, and he projects authority on to representatives of the public. In this process the public domain becomes peopled with personal demons. (All men do this in their need to render familiar what is other, but within a reciprocal exchange process between subject and object which ensures that demons be either tamed or caged as rowdy, incompatible guests.) On the one hand, what is external is regarded as threatening and therefore evil, operating at an uncontrollable distance, beyond mediation. On the other hand, paradoxically, private and public are confused, so that all distance collapses in the projection of the inner world on to external phenomena. The ways the Puritan established for relating private to public have broken down, leaving a chasm.

In the paranoid key Puritan virtues are cancelled. For instance, self-consciousness is impossible. The paranoid denies his self in a process that endows, quite gratuitously, other beings with his own more destructive forces. By definition, he can have no in-sight. Life is conducted on an infantile battlefield in which the individual's sole preoccupation is to destroy threatening forces before they destroy him. The strategy of self-understanding has no role in this struggle to break besieging anxiety.

Second, there is no possibility of 'responsible' action in Puritan terms. Responsibility requires distance, self-understanding and control. For the paranoid it is always someone else who is to blame. Misfortune, like all emotional states and influences, comes from without. Even sin is projected: hence the paranoid's chronic fear of the unknown, his lack of curiosity and his one-dimensional imagination. The paranoid accepts the existence of authority, but in a negative, punitive form. He lives the antithesis of personal responsibility; having no self, it is the external that is always guilty.

Paranoia may also be diagnosed in less obvious cases. The impulse that all men feel at times to seek explanations for what they have done reflects an insecurity at the wellsprings of individual action, a fear that they have blundered and must defend themselves before some grand, omnipresent, supra-individual court of justice. Shame, in this case, lies at the root of paranoid responses. The Puritan fear of being stained might thus be taken in part as paranoid - that is, to the degree that the court is supra-individual.

However, in this essay, the term 'paranoia' will be applied only to situations in which an individual greatly and irrationally exaggerates threats on the private from the public, that is, situations in which the threat is conceived of in such a way that he endows the external with power and complexity, to the neglect of his private, inner world. In some of the cases to be discussed this classical type of paranoia, characterized by delusions of persecution, is complemented by the other classical type, characterized by delusions of grandeur, that is, by exaggerated perceptions of self-importance and personal power.

On a social level, paranoid tendencies are most obviously present in political attitudes, and, in particular, in conspiracy theories. As Karl Popper has pointed out in some detail, the blaming habit - prototype of the paranoid - has been prominent in the Marxist socialist tradition. On the right, paranoia has carried a further symptom, not always a part of extremism of the left. McCarthyism in the USA illustrates the phenomenon of the individual through projective identification seeing persecution and conspiracy focused not against

himself directly but against the virtuous group or nation. He then
has all the more grounds, as an altruistic crusader, for righteous
indignation.

What might be termed 'paranoid social theory' is characterized
by simple, all-encompassing explanations for complex events; by
the moralizing of social behaviour into good and evil; and by a
millennial belief that social life would be transformed immediately
after the overthrow of key power interests. I include with the third
quality the complementary paranoia of the reactionary, who fears
that change would precipitate a millennial hell.

A strict relativist might object to the term 'paranoia' on the
grounds that to use it assumes a notion of 'reality'. Who is to say
what is real? This response, common in the last decade, is founded
on two old confusions. The relativist falsely assumes that the 'realist'
in claiming an order of things takes that order to be absolute, either
in terms of moral worth or historical continuity. The realist may
legitimately claim that there are economic, social and psychological
laws governing the manifest action of men and institutions.
Certainly whether these laws be good, evil or neutral depends on the
largely independent evaluations of individuals; and these laws have
without exception a culturally relative dimension, evolving through
time and space. But at any given historical moment there are
impulses, necessities, patterns, with their origins in past, present
and future, that govern human behaviour, and may to a certain
degree be interpreted. In sum, the person who believes that anyone
who approaches him intends kidnap is paranoid; so is he in the West
who believes that the 'big brother' corporate state is watching him.
Moreover, there is a characteristic psychological irony in the fact that
the relativist's very denial of 'reality' is paranoid, disclosing a
projection on to the realist of his own incapacity to think in
non-absolute categories.

The debate between relativism and realism centres on different
notions of change. My assumption in this essay is that both character
and society change very slowly. Therefore it is paranoid in a further
sense to stake judgments on an overestimation of the velocity of an
individual's psychological disposition.

Another paranoid characteristic is manifest in contemporary radical
politics, which is prevalently socialist or anarchist. The poor,
under-privileged, deviant or insane classes are endowed with

extraordinary powers of latent virtue, uniquely capable of redeeming society from incipient decay. (The notion of the *Volk* played the identical role for Nazi ideology.) The research of political sociology, vindicating Pareto's hypothesis that élites are endemic to society, reveals vacuously utopian this neo franciscan attempt to invert Calvin's doctrine of election.

Weber asserted how very rarely it happens that political action is more than the public exhibition and attempted resolution of private vicissitudes (or, in my terms, more than a paranoid technique for bolstering the individual ego). Groping for some absolute criteria for judging political conduct, he concluded by offering that he found it deeply moving to observe that rare case in which a man's public actions are governed by the rationality that is only possible within the framework of an ethic of ultimate individual responsibility. His peculiarly Puritan call was for a politics which was passionate, and yet in which projections would be self-reflectively controlled.

We have arrived at the point of entry into an argument that would contrast Puritan and paranoid politics, finding the former, at its best, to be exemplary. But an exemplary politics may no longer be relevant: remissive culture requires that politics be replaced by administration, for individual authority has no function in a culture geared to stimulating and satisfying an ever-proliferating range of desires. (One corollary is that the academic discipline of political science be replaced by sociology.) It may be that Weber's disquisitions into political ethics were no more than one of the most intellectually powerful spasms of a dying culture.

The paranoid represents a transition phase from Puritan to remissive cultures.

3

The Remissive

In the remissive culture the sins of the fathers are no more, or so it is believed. Relieved of their burden the remitted man is free to live his fancied ideology, which is hedonist. Ideally guilt no longer binds: the driving dynamic of the culture provides a plethora of techniques for remission, for release from internalized constraint.

The concept of the 'remissive' employed here borrows from Philip Rieff's concept of the 'therapeutic', which he develops in his second book, *The Triumph of the Therapeutic: Uses of Faith after Freud*. I have decided against retaining 'therapeutic' as the designation for the emerging culture, because of its common connotations of healing. One should not exaggerate the hospital so that it becomes the pivotal institution of contemporary life. The metaphor is powerful, but not exclusively valid. Only one of the remission strategies is psychotherapy, Freudian or otherwise. What is more generally involved in the Puritan nature striving to live hedonistically is the remission of sins, the achievement of a state of grace characterized, not by spirituality, but by the availability to pleasure.

The culture under scrutiny is drawn by hedonist aspirations and has as its principal task release from inherited guilt. Commonly, though, it achieves only an aimless and unimpassioned meandering after pleasure. The remitted man is a depressive Dionysus, drained of ecstatic fury, seemingly more gutted than remitted; in his ways he is remiss.

The remissive culture's intellectual father was Freud. Not Freud the patriarch, whose personal identifications were more with great protagonists of control (such as Cromwell and Moses), but rather Freud the therapist, whose endeavour is a powerful argument, as Rieff phrases it, 'for expressive remissions from failed controls, restabilizing the moral demands that are culture at a fresh locus of imbalance between controls and remissions'. (It is not anomalous that our remissive culture, particularly its American strain, has generated numerous attempts in recent years to recreate religious commitments, notably by the generation of youth. The epidemic and unascetically vicarious nature of these impulses in search of faith suggests that they fulfil the role more of one type of pleasure, with its logic of diminishing emotional returns with prolonged indulgence, than a resurgence of the pious pursuit of salvation characteristic of serious religious commitment.)

Freud, like Nietzsche, spanned the old and the new cultures: both men were temperamentally Puritan, and yet did more than any other individuals to build theoretical weapons that would eventually succeed in demolishing the Protestant ethos that was the psychological engine of the old culture. While Freud did seek to engineer releases from over-severe individual and cultural superegos, he never favoured instinctual abandon. His therapeutic goal was to achieve a better balance between individual desire and the prohibitions of culture, a greater control of anxiety and a greater capacity for bearing uncertainty. His emphasis rests on control, on non-neurotic renunciation, on gratifying sublimation. Moreover, nobody has taught us more decisively just how binding is the past. On the subject of child development, Freud commented, 'in mental life nothing which has once been formed can perish'. (One of the favourite dictums of seventeenth-century New England Puritans was 'God has so cast the line of election that for the most part it runs through the loins of godly parents'.) By and large Freud reaffirmed the central principles of the old culture, in which releases were built into controls, in which desires were sublimated in love and work; he rejected both therapies of commitment (new attempts to find faith) and therapies of pure release. At the same time his onerous therapy demanded strong commitment from the patient, a faith in the healing power of intellect and knowledge which looks more and more anachronistic to today's therapy-seekers.

The remissive culture is prescriptively anti-moralist. In a moralist culture, like the Puritan, conflicts are resolved between society's demands and an individual's desires by the enforcement of prohibitions; undisputed norms governing conduct act as palliatives for panic and despair. The remissive-hedonist's one conscious norm is to be anti-Puritan, to abide by a symbolic of anarchist moral demands - slack commands to disregard norms - to doubt all inherited values, to deny the primacy of any particular organization and personality. This state is one of 'permanent cultural revolution', with the proviso that too vigorous an assault on the old structures of order is neurotic, symptomatic of taking those orders too seriously, not being adequately emancipated from them.

But this amoralism represents the remissive's view of himself rather than any reality. A remissive style is necessarily normative, approving of spontaneity, intimacy, hedonist release, emotional openness, disapproving of authority and control, reproachful of the stance of reproach. It sets up its own logic of control and release - one of its controls is an ideology of release. In the case of the mature remissive this moralism is impeccably tacit, the tolerance ethic so well internalized that aggression manifests itself only in his responding with relatively less enthusiasm to gentiles. However, in that this moralism is concealed under a veiling image of normlessness, it is more insidious, and more coercive than Puritan intolerance, which operates from within that framework of controlled explicitness which a commitment to honesty and responsibility enforces.

The problem that crucially determines a society's viability is that of maintaining a tolerable, integrating balance between the private psychological needs of its individuals and the requirements of its administering political and economic institutions. The thesis argued here is that this general rule transforms into the following particular in the case of contemporary Western society: that the cardinal socio-cultural problem (leaving aside looming socio-economic problems of scarce resources) is how individuals with inherently Puritan character dispositions can adapt to their chosen hedonist ideology.

Every culture has two main functions: first, to constitute the process of symbol formation and utilization by which the individual, obeying an indigenous drive, makes objectively actual his inner core of potential subjective perfection (Simmel); second, to ensure that the moral demands men make upon themselves enable the collectivities to which they belong to function as viable economic, social and military entities, and to organize those demands into a system of symbols that makes men intelligible and, in particular, predictable to each other, thus also rendering the world intelligible (Machiavelli, Durkheim, Rieff). The rising situation is one in which the latter function is fulfilled by the remissive-hedonist ideology (although we may have doubts about its contribution to military viability). Men are coming to perceive each other in terms of service and welfare, of mutual remission. As much in the economic as in the personal domain, the tissues of contemporary solidarity are drawn from the new ideology. Tensions that the individual experiences as a result of failures of culture in its first function are eased through tactics in remission.

But as the remissive ideology becomes pervasive, displacing Puritan morality, those with Puritan dispositions will find greater difficulty of personal expression. The presiding symbolic will only deny or distort their subjective potential. For them culture fails in its first function.

The ensuing cultural conflict generates tensions from which the individual must find relief. Three distinct reactions are possible: first, that of the conservative, who resists the new culture in reaffirming the old; second, that of the remissive-hedonist, the most pragmatic of the three, who sees that what constrains him from measuring up to his ideals is his own character, from which he must gain remission; third, that of the paranoid, who represses recognition of the internalized presence of the old culture, of disposition, and devotes himself with revolutionary zeal to living the style of the new.

There is a fourth possibility, lying somewhere between the first and the second: that of the individual recognizing his neo-Puritan disposition and setting himself a synthetic Puritan-remissive ideology. Further discussion of this reaction is postponed.

At the moral level, remission represents forgiveness of all sins; at the instinctual level, release from all controls. The inheritance of commitments to a forbidding ethos, the base from which ascetic Christianity established its cultural hegemony in the West, has been placed under sustained assault from the alternative ethical strain in the original Christian doctrine, that of a forgiving pathos. Objective grounds for guilt are being abolished; no one and nothing is to blame, the only responsibility borne by the individual is that he choose his pleasures successfully. The Puritan gods of ascetic control, sensual renunciation, and high sublimation, are giving way to the pagan anti-god of polymorphous perversity, of prolific, uncensored indulgence of impulse. Metaphysical achievements have not lost all their appeal; but they have lost their monopoly on human dignity, and joined ranks with the physical. This is summed up in Rieff's claim that modern satisfaction really consists in a consoling plenitude of option.

The emerging hedonist ideology had as its necessary, but not obviously sufficient, generative condition the economic changes within advancing industrial societies that occurred in the first half of this century. At the level of consumption, increasing production *per capita* and an associated comparative expansion of the tertiary or service sector of the economy brought with it a rapidly mounting need for greater consumer demand. The answer to this need depended on the consumer living more hedonistically, learning the potentially inexhaustible pleasure of purchasing novelty, and scrapping it at whim. At the level of production, increasing degrees of mechanization and automation have made industry progressively less labour-intensive, and have correspondingly reduced institutional dependence on the Puritan work ethic.

The question arises as to why economic structures should have changed at a faster rate than character. The answer exemplifies what Simmel described as the tragedy of culture: that individuals of a particular disposition, in this case Puritan, create social forms which then proceed to obey an alien, objective logic all their own, and no longer mediate those culture-creating individuals to themselves. So it happened that an institutional structure was established which eventually would make the heirs of its founding fathers redundant. While a manifold of profound changes has occurred since the seventeenth century in both the domains of character and of society, it is largely in this century that the divorce of character from its evolving social function has been thrown into heavy relief.

The utilitarian ethic, which originally governed the endeavours of economic man, has been drawn out of its materialist confines to provide remissive-hedonist man with an analogous pleasure-principle. Social activity remains governed by the same maximization formulae, but the indices are multiplied. Western society may still be characterized by its pursuit of improved techniques of economic supply: the concept 'technology' has merely been widened to include remissive devices, manufactured across the entire spectrum of the economy, from the most capital-intensive of the consumer-goods industries to the knowledge industries. The expanded technology enables a plethora of remissive activities ranging from automobile games to indulgence in psychological medicine. Moreover, the elevation of economic progress to a position of superiority over alternative social and political goals has placed the remissive and its service ethic at the fulcrum of social process.

But economic man was renunciative, anally-retentive and Puritan, whereas remissive man is appetitive, orally-indulgent and in many ways *Catholic*. The axiom of psychoanalysis that to talk honestly is to exorcize all guilt mirrors the Catholic confessional: there are no sins once they have been confessed in penitence. Any distance between the patient and the all-forgiving mother Church can theoretically be eliminated. The remissive equivalent to the Church is modern society itself, and its concern with pathos, which unlike character is not bound by its past.

Freud would not agree that men's desires are free from the past determination of individual character, a determination both inherited from earlier generations and impressed in first childhood. Believing with the Puritan in original sin, he aimed no higher than he found practical, to ease slightly the pressure of guilt. But a different psychoanalysis, adopting a Rousseauist optimism about possibilities for casting off the burdensome past, has installed itself at the doctrinal centre of the remissive culture. Those who remain uncomfortable in their pleasures take their *dis-ease* to Wilhelm Reich, to the therapists of Esalen in California, or to the 'primal scream' engineer, Janov, all of whom unambivalently concentrate on instinctual release: Freud's complex intellectual ploys to reinforce the weaponry of ego have given way to various techniques for physical massage.

The Puritan regarded his sin as his own private affair, to be handled by himself; but for the Catholic what is hidden from confession damns. The sluice-gates between private and public that Puritanism had erected are slowly opening. It is a secularized Catholicism that returns, substituting an ethic of tolerance and forgiveness for the Puritan ethic of perfection and unredeemable culpability. With the availability of public consolation there lapses the imperative that the individual strive continuously to illustrate his god-like perfection. He is no longer moved by pride, a quality of character rather than emotion; he becomes indifferent to excellence, arriving at the Catholic recognition that not being perfect he will live best by taking pleasure in his imperfections.

Better to pursue his own clumsy crafts, and enjoy his playful dabbling, than stand always in awe before the works of Olympian genius. (Counterbalancing the expansion of the giant corporation and the mass-produced commodity, producers and consumers have shown a developing taste in advanced industrial societies for the output of diverse, small, neo-artisan industries. But whereas there is some demand that goods be of quality, traditions of excellence which were established by the trained and dedicated discipline of European craftsmen are being maintained only in rare cases, such as *haute couture* - a craft which may not require stringently ascetic commitments.)

Where Puritan piety endures, notably in the phenomenon of concentrated reverence for the self, it is divested of its shame-sensibility, and is abstracted from communal projects. The 'public' is no longer a focus for individual interest; in its modern guise as the industrial state, the complex of institutions that service the remissive's pleasures, it bears none of the interdictory sanctions that once issued from the city fathers. The individual, finding the traditional sphere of the public ethically-neutral, turned his interest to his own subjective world as the locus for meaningful reflection on human conduct. (Recent attempts to revalue the public by accusing it of environmental pollution and racial discrimination will not restore the political arena as the stage for ethical debate; indeed these are rather criticisms of the public for mismanagement, failing to administer according to its mandate, which is to maximize community welfare. In the first case, it was failing to take account of the long-term maintenance of pleasure, in the second it was restricting the access of certain sections of the population to the fruits of affluence.)

The ascetic pursuit of salvation places the psychological demand on the Puritan that he never do anything for its own sake. When he plays, it is with utmost seriousness. Time must be used frugally, not wasted on passing pleasures; each act must constitute a milestone passed on the road to salvation. A surrogate form of this Puritan instrumentalism is generated by the sage ethic, and its non-ludic first principle, according to which the individual is justified in indulging in any new experience as a means for gaining wider *knowledge* of life, and hence wisdom. A remissive culture, by contrast, has lost faith in salvation, and in its substitutes such as truth and wisdom. It values knowledge in two senses: as functionally necessary for technological progress, or as the prize competed for in pleasurable intellectual games. Knowledge is not pursued with religious seriousness: ultimate meaning is not at stake.

Even the Greek fatalist tradition, with its scorn for transcendental strivings, and its warnings against hubris, had closer affinities with the Puritan than with the remissive. Life was not conceived of as the random pursuit of pleasure; rather it contained inherent meaning, it unfolded according to the set pattern of fate, each act within it reflecting a predetermined transcendent design. This perspective was explicit from *The Iliad* to *Oedipus the King*. The remissive, by contrast, emphasizes choice, indeterminacy and the vacuity of metaphysics - whether of a mystical, cosmological or ethical bent.

Puritanism's commitment to vocation does not preclude 'play' as a cultural process. There is Puritan play, deep play, but in the restricted sense that Freud spelt out, as a means for expressing inner conflict and drama, as form-endowing sublimation, as passion's channelling performance and catharsis. Thus culture's first function is played out. In any society, moreover, there is a second source of conflict threatening the individual, one associated with culture's second function, that of providing a symbolic whose function is to integrate the community; this conflict also must be played out. The general morality of the community will inevitably be hostile at times to the individual's wishes; then it is through participating in collective rituals that that individual plays out his private frustration, and regains faith in the legitimacy of the community's values. In this sense Puritans, like all social beings, participate in play. However, the Puritan's sense of salvation orients him with greater commitment to culture's first function, and, in association, to play as a private pursuit.

The hallmark of passion is the endurance of gratified desire; desire that does not wane on indulgence. The teleology of passion inevitably involves salvation, mystical union or truth, never merely happiness or pleasure. Tristan, Macbeth serving his ambition, Phèdre, Werther, and Flaubert's Frédéric Moreau are heroes of passion; Camus's Meursault is their anti-hero. A remissive culture is indifferent to passion.

The Puritan has a paradigmatically passionate character. Passion takes different forms. For Hester Prynne, for example, it takes the form of romance, in the tradition of Tristan. For other Puritans it takes the form of work. They are 'called' to their work; and to work according to a calling requires trained relentlessness and single-minded absorption, lack of interest in other activity, particularly in the ephemeral and the sensual: this is the sustained asceticism characteristic of true passion. One of Friedrich Nietzsche's aphorisms is suggestive of his own Puritan sensibility: 'Not the intensity but the duration of high feelings makes high men.'

Beyond romance and work, passion runs in less obvious channels. In particular, a sense of individual authority, the cultivation of ethos, requires an enduring commitment to an order of personality scrupulously built according to a blueprint of moral commands. Historically, a decline in this type of authority, when it is not replaced by abiding attachments to alternative codes of meaning like a nation, a church, an aesthetic culture or a hermetic commune, indicates a general waning of passion. Indeed, in retrospect, the ethical framework of Puritan culture appears to have provided the last vehicle in the West capable of supporting the ascetic demands of our archetype of passion.

'Pleasure', in its modern, utilitarian usage, usually means pleasing the senses, and carries with it a release from emotional restraint. Modern pleasure is independent of anything noumenal, and contrasts with joy and ecstasy in that it does not conform to the paradigm of passion. (Men who live by passion find full release only in death.)

To pursue pleasure in a modern, remissive manner is to pursue comfort. And to seek comfort is to evade sustained intensity, ecstasy and anguish, the central attributes of passion. Indeed, comfort, beneath its surface of material ease, is the primary antidote to what in the first Tristan myth was the potion which catalyses passion. (In the pre-Puritan world of this version of the myth the passion of love was not viewed as natural. The action of a magical, external agent, a love potion, was required to take man out of his ordinary senses, into passion.)

Both culture and age influence the forms in which an individual conceptualizes pleasure. In a hedonism-oriented culture the old will have a biologically determined preference for pleasure in the form of comfort, whereas the young will likely have a leaning towards more active, impulsive, even quasi-dangerous, pastimes.

The original Freudian endeavour was governed by mixed motives. Psychoanalysis was inaugurated as a new tool in the

European individual's search for truth and in particular for self-understanding. At this level, like the psychological philosophy of Nietzsche, it obeyed the Puritan passion paradigm. However, psychoanalysis was also designed to cure, in the specific sense of relaxing tension, loosening the collar of anxiety, and easing intolerable burdens of misery. In this it operated in the service of the pleasure principle, offering the individual new strategies for release. The remissive has tended to forget psychoanalysis's passionate search and remembered only its second, cure, function.

The distinction between passion and pleasure, here as elsewhere, is not as clear cut as has so far been suggested. Introspection that is directed at the end of self-knowledge, and is not employed as a means for escaping from the both constraining and enabling cage of character, represents one of the important Puritan activities. Milton's hope for the fallen Adam was for 'A paradise within thee, happier far'. If the Puritan *uses* his self-knowledge, he does so for the better control of his delinquent impulses, or as a means of consolation for having to bear an inexorably difficult fate. Pleasure may be gained from either of these applications, but it is pleasure subordinate to and derivative from the achievement of ascetic goals. It would be convenient for the argument to be able to identify this pleasure as joy or tranquillity, in contrast with the fruits of a more directly sensual hedonism. There is something to this distinction, but only imprecisely.

The significant distinction lies with the context in which pleasure is derived. The Puritan derives pleasure from successful self-projection into works which then gain an enduring life of their own. He fulfils himself by establishing ethos, creating perfect forms. His allegiance is to the structure, the artifact or the style, not to the pleasure itself. In the remissive's paradigm of pleasure, ethos or self are trivial in themselves; they serve at the most as instruments to be dropped after the moment of release.

Concern with self as such, as a highly differentiated entity, is out of place in a remissive culture. Pleasure is the escape from self through sensual abandon. (The noumenal abandon of the Buddhist is another matter.) Freud's remission-bonded followers have been increasingly less interested in constructing complex, conceptually sophisticated models of personality than the master himself. Laing's loosely grounded theory of 'ontological insecurity', 'true and false self', capitalizing on popular existentialist distinctions, illustrates this decline in the passion for rigorous self-understanding. The attempt to fuse existentialism with psychoanalysis (Jaspers, Binswanger, Laing and numerous Americans), to focus analysis on the 'self', was important as a means for defusing the Puritan component in Freud's psychological man. The analytical session was transformed into the informal personal visit, with emphasis shifted from theory and interpretation to a more friendly exploration of the nuances of spontaneous feeling connecting patient to therapist.

Concern with the existential self plays a transitional role in the emergence of the remissive. An obvious first step in self-detachment from the interdicts of external culture is to invest the self with supreme authority. But such a move takes on passionate dimensions only for the type Rieff has called 'psychological man', who is an uncommon individual in the remissive culture. For the majority, the defusing of authority leads to the end of an absorbing interest in the complexities of ego, and to an inundation by the tide of polymorphous pleasure. It is significant that recent decades have seen the final exhaustion of the intellectual movements that philosophically and psychologically served to advance our understanding of the self, existentialism-phenomenology and psychoanalysis. We find today that the quintessentially remissive 'counter-culture' singles out 'ego-tripping' as destructive, indicating a movement into a purer remissive mode, beyond existentialist concerns. Rieff's 'psychological man' is already a type of the past; his Puritan faith in inner knowledge about a structured personality is virtually extinct amongst the latest generations of university students.

At this point Camus's novel *L'Etranger* (1942) merits attention, for its leading themes interweave vestiges of Puritan morality with the mentality of the remissive, and with hedonism. The hero, Meursault, lives what is essentially the hedonist ideology: Camus writes elsewhere that

> in Algiers, for those who are young and alive, everything is their haven and an occasion for excelling - the bay, the sun, the red and white checkerboard of terraces going down to the sea, the flowers and stadiums, the fresh brown bodies.

Here are embodied the pleasure values that form the remissive character-type's guiding ideology, ones popularized in a moralistic form in America from the late 1960s by such celebrated works as

Charles Reich's *The Greening of America* (1970).

But the sun-loving Meursault is often bored; he neglects himself at home. He shows little capacity for human attachment or intimacy; his hedonism is at best episodic. His intermittency of spirit suggests not spontaneity but repression, an incapacity for emotional response first exhibited in his seeming indifference to his mother's death. He himself supplies the clue to his behaviour when he tells his lawyer that 'all normal people had more or less desired the death of those they loved, at some time or other'. The repressed returns: under conditions of extreme heat, conditions that he associates with his mother's funeral, he murders an innocent Arab. Camus underlines the point by having Meursault discover in prison a story of a mother 'slaughtering' her son 'with a hammer' - thus vindicating Meursault's own matricidal impulse. Appropriately the trial prosecutor asserts that Meursault was a criminal from the time of his mother's funeral.

Meursault managed to live his hedonism part-time, until Puritan vestiges of guilt surfaced, precipitated by his mother's death. For him remission is not available. Yet he reflects in the novel's last paragraph that nobody had any right to weep for his mother, for at the end she had been on the brink of choosing a fiancé, finding freedom and solace in the dusk. His final recognition, that his mother was about to discover a dignity and hope in that very hedonism that had been his *modus vivendi*, generates in Meursault sympathy for another human being that he had not hitherto shown. In this moment, with punishment imminent, he gains a kind of absolution, and happiness.

Meursault is an imperfect type of the remissive-hedonist. He is more successful in his hedonism, or at least his hedonism is more grounded in practice, less merely an ideology. Accordingly, unlike contemporary Western Puritans in search of deconversion, he is unmoralistic. Without zeal or ideals, he does not pursue remission. But he has a binding past, which destroys him. If anything he exhibits a paranoid response to cultural conflict by repressing recognition of the internalized presence of the old culture and devoting himself solely to the new. It so happens, however, that in his case repression surfaces as depressive indolence rather than as paranoid moralism.

The vast majority within Western societies have to date few consolidated points of contact with the remissive. The emerging remissive culture shows its dominance so far mainly in the domain of ideology. But communities are like individuals in their need for a lengthy, sometimes interminable, gestation period before they can fully accommodate the practical reality of how they live to their ideals. Moreover, just as an achieved state of mature capitalism was for Marx prerequisite for the communist revolution, so a society must be fully bourgeois before it will, and then of its own nature, transform into the totally remissive mode. To date the life-style of remissive-hedonist man remains largely a bourgeois luxury.

4

The Decline of
Individual Authority

The old social order, founded psychologically on interdictory-renunciatory modes of resolving conflict between instinct and culture, is giving way to the remissive-indulgent mode. In this section my aim is to examine the transition by considering themes that relate to 'authority', to its changing images and manifestations.

Persons, groups, institutions, governments have 'authority' when others voluntarily recognize their right to decide, to command, to judge, to organize, or simply to exist unchallenged as they are. Authority often depends on the ability, if necessary, to sanction commands by means of economic power, or ultimately of physical violence. But an individual may have charismatic authority by virtue of his power of speech, or of the force of his personality. An institution may have authority by virtue of tradition, of its past record. I do not wish to attempt a precise definition of 'authority'. I am reluctant to tamper with its common-sense connotations, preferring their ungainly amalgam of manifold hints and insistencies. Hopefully, the argument to follow will make the charge I read in this elusive concept adequately visible.

People from diverse segments of society have, this century, argued that authority is in general decline. This is not quite so. Authority will not be completely extinct in the pure state of the remissive. What we are currently experiencing is certainly the decline of individual authority; but overall the nature of authority is changing rather than being eliminated. Authority's presence is being reduced along only one of its two major dimensions.

In the Puritan culture, individual authority had two projections: it ruled the private world of character through the ethics of responsibility and honesty, and it ruled the public world through the manifestation of the same virtues in politics and administration.

Its demise has had different consequences in the two domains. First, as Rieff suggests, the private is being taken over by the remissive mode according to which nothing is secret or sinful, nothing forbidden and consequently nothing authoritative, at either a social or an individual level. Thus the pleasure principle engulfs all competing ethics. Second, however, in the public domain, the erosion of the Protestant ethic has been paralleled by the gargantuan proliferation, to a degree unforeseen even by Marx, in individual size and overall range of practice, of bureaucratically organized institutions. The power of these institutions today is inestimable. They directly control patterns of work, leisure and consumption; they indirectly influence all spheres of social life from the decisions of governments to the constitution of families. The power to influence carries with it authority. Moreover, once institutions are established they gain a second type of authority, that of tradition: they come to belong to the perceived order of things, which is endowed with an innate legitimacy. To challenge them, then, is to threaten the deeper layers of the social order.

Weber prophesied in 1918 that only a charismatic leader of demonic megalomania would divert, and then temporarily, the inevitable course of industrial society's omnivorous determination of every aspect of modern life. This grim course was already too far advanced for rational individuals to control. Here is fertile soil for a Marxist interpretation of the decline of individual authority, as merely the private reflection of an irreversible economic process. In what Galbraith has called the 'new industrial state' there is no place for charismatic leaders, for men of personality imposing their individual print on their public interests. In Weber's time individual entrepreneurs were still prominent; the public celebrity of a Henry Ford reflected the power that such an individual wielded. Today the names of the chairmen or managing directors of even the largest corporations are unknown: as administrators working with set goals and set techniques these men are immediately replaceable. It is collectivities themselves - ministries, corporations, trade unions and various interest groups - that now have authority. Moreover, managers in every type of organization have lost more than individual distinction: their work is more and more controlled by government regulation; they themselves are more and more supervised by government regulators. Economics itself has taken on the features of the remissive, no longer providing the arena in which captains of industry might prove themselves; its image is now that of fuel source for pleasure rather than the coliseum for character; work becomes a means for providing greater pleasure, and when it is more than that it is as a pleasure itself. As Marx would have suggested, this trend is a function of advancing industrialization.

The economic example carries over into other spheres of public life. Yesterday's statesmen and city fathers have been replaced by today's administrators, social engineers and accountants. There is no longer any effective call for that sense of civic duty, of selfless and thoughtful work for the community, or the nation, that was one of the great achievements of Puritan culture, notably in the United States (although many observers lament its absence). In sum, whatever the precise relationship between the decline of individual authority and changing economic structures, there is a strong 'affinity', to use Weber and Merleau-Ponty's historiographic term, between the two processes.

The élite which manage the industrial state provide but one example of the declining significance of the individual. Authority has shifted to the institutions themselves. Individuals still have a public role only at the political margins where they form pressure groups bent on remedying the system's malfunctions (such as poverty and pollution). But these roles too are rapidly institutionalized in the form of small 'watch-dog' government departments. Charisma, emptied of character and created as 'image', is now the preserve of mass media entertainers. Authority may exist in the domain of economics, and in that rare politics which is more than pure theatre, but it is of the legalistic type. (Tocqueville prophesied that it was in the nature of American democracy to produce national leaders of chilling mediocrity.)

The Puritan, in his guise of *homo economicus*, was the architect and financier of the industrial revolution. This revolution was achieved largely in the secondary sector of the economy, that of manufacturing; it involved the initial development of heavy, capital-goods industries such as steel, and subsequently a slow displacement of investment into consumer-goods industries. This revolution was won when the industrial base became large enough to supply, if required, every member of society with a standard of living comfortably above the subsistence level. With that victory such Puritan traits as frugality lost much of their economic utility: for by this stage the advanced capitalist economy was operating in

the main through large institutions where the functions of owner
and manager had been separated, the manager deciding the rules
for capital formation and investment. This system was no longer
dependent on individual entrepreneurs saving their profits in order
to reinvest them, rather than spending them on private luxuries.

We are now experiencing a second revolution, one which has
been termed variously post-industrial, post-capitalist, consumer,
technetronic. It is being achieved in the tertiary sector of the
economy, in what are called, significantly, the service-industries.
The heavy industrial infrastructure, supplemented in recent
decades by innovations in automation, is large enough to provide
high levels of consumer affluence. The issues of the second
economic revolution are what types of affluence should be planned
and how that affluence should be distributed. This power of the
Midas touch has progressively reduced the work-load borne by
human labour whilst it has progressively increased the product
available to that labour for diversifying its leisure pastime. In short,
economic change has prepared the way for the life-styles of the
remissive culture, although not as quickly as many recent prophets
of change have forecast.

Moreover, it is the stability created by the advanced industrial
economy, with its high degree of authority over its inputs of labour
and capital and its output product, that has made the remissive
mode possible. Otherwise the anomic erosion of the old constraints
would, as in the past, have led to a state of Hobbesian insecurity,
forcing in turn new constraints and methods of policing them in
order to limit an intolerable anarchy. The unassailable, ubiquitous,
although often covert, authority of the public domain today is a key
enabling factor in the decline of authority in the private. One
corollary is that the remissive individual does not enjoy the
untrammelled polymorphous pleasures of *l'homme naturel*, but
technologically-mediated releases under the often faint but
nevertheless binding controls of their heavily structured socio-
economic context.

Economic change has been complemented by shifts in patterns of
family socialization. Many commentators have claimed that the
direction of change, especially in middle-class families, is towards a
greater recognition of the child's wants; whether this is what occurs,
child-rearing strategies that reinforced orally-retentive behaviour
have given way to those that support the orally-indulgent. The

patriarchal, disciplinarian methods which produced the strictly self-controlled adults suitable for the Puritan economy have been relaxed. The popularity in recent decades of handbooks of child-rearing that stress parental permissiveness, whatever their actual influence, is illustrative of the remissive aspirations of mothers.

Running parallel with these transformations in political and economic authority went radical changes in Western epistemology, in the authority of knowledge. Since the Enlightenment three distinctive phases can be distinguished from among the manifold of reformations, counter-reformations and new heresies which have pulsed through Europe. First, the positivist tradition with its confidence in the indubitable power of deductive-empirical science, its dissociation of knowledge from ethics and disregard of the latter. Second, the subjectivist reaction, posited by Nietzsche and Dilthey, deepened in the work of Freud, finally developed in the transcendental subjectivism of Husserl, Heidegger, Merleau-Ponty and their followers. Third, epistemological nihilism, in which all and conversely nothing is permitted as non-trivial, reliable knowledge.

Puritanism has played a split role in this genealogy. In its attachment to the power of rigorous and sustained intellect, applied to this-worldly affairs, it played a considerable part in the rise of positivist objectivism, and in particular its contribution to economic science and practice. On the other hand, that same intellectualism combined with the alternative Puritan drive towards inwardness to promote a more subjectivist philosophy. Both Hegel and Nietzsche claimed that German philosophy was merely an off-shoot of the Protestant religion.

Kant, himself the product of a Protestant pietist background, following Hume, laid the ground for subjectivist epistemology. Moreover, in his denial of the possibility of knowing the thing-in-itself, and his consequent emphasis on 'appearance', there was a strong anti-positivist strain. Hegel's dialectical philosophy went further, denying the Aristotelian notion of truth based on the law of non-contradiction. But it was only with Nietzsche's attack on the psychological roots of knowledge, his rejection of the thing-in-itself, and his assertion that we construct rather than discover truths, which are in fact convenient fictions or illusions employed by the individual for the purpose of self-justification, that is merely subjective perspectives, that the authority of objective knowledge was pervasively undermined.

Nietzsche, the first outstanding 'psychological man', attempted to institute a method of self-reflective thinking to replace both empirical positivism and Romantic idealism. His aim was a self-knowledge that would penetrate the individual's preconceptions about himself, those idealizing fantasies that protected him from exploring the more precarious regions of his personality. But this knowledge was also to cancel itself as it proceeded, in order to ensure that the thinking individual never succumbed to the objectivist illusion of having a permanently true image of himself, of carving himself as a deadly static idol. Nietzsche provided the spark for the rage against positivism. At the same time he sought to found a knowledge that would have authority in the domain of the individual's psychological self-reflections. He, nevertheless, as Heidegger has pointed out at length, prepared the way for epistemological nihilism.

Freud's work, although hardly philosophical in itself, provided the Nietzschean endeavour with a firm empirical basis. Psychological self-knowledge was underpinned with a sophisticated theory grounded in case-studies. Out of this work emerged psychological man, as yet with a Puritan dedication to rigorous intellect, and a preference for the pursuit of inner truth over that of immediate pleasure.

Contemporaneously, Husserl was developing his philosophical system of transcendental subjectivism. He brought about in philosophical terms what the emerging psychology had achieved in its own way, to place the individual self at the centre of all enquiry. He took as the locus for all knowledge the individual *cogito* and meditated on how, working by means of empathy and analogy, it constitutes its own external world in the form of cogitations. He sought to take all knowledge back to the first principle of the individual ego transcending itself through thinking. Phenomenological philosophy was to be grounded ultimately in 'all-embracing self-investigation': it took the objective world as real only in the situating role it plays in the thinking-process. Husserl balanced his cautious, rationalist ambition to work meticulously through reason's possibilities with occasional aphorisms: he closed his *Cartesian Meditations* with Augustine's command: 'Do not wish to go out; go back into yourself. Truth dwells in the inner man.'

Heidegger took the next step towards epistemological nihilism, by comparatively disregarding the transcendental subject. But knowledge retains authority: learning to think in the new manner Heidegger spells out requires great self-discipline, a shunning of the plans and business of the practical everyday world, an overcoming of impulses to strive, in order to attain the state of trained *Gelassenheit* that is prerequisite to knowledge. Heidegger preserves an absolute first principle, not the individual ego but 'Being', that of which the particular entity is an occurrence. He staves off nihilism by moving into a mystical metaphysics.

Since Dilthey there have been a number of attempts in the human sciences to combine subjectivist and positivist methods. Weber's *verstehende Soziologie* and the diverse work of the Frankfurt School stand out.

The knowledge relevant to the remissive is prescriptively without authority: its function is to please, not to command or even to instruct. It has neither the authority of serving an absolute first principle about which it provides insights, themselves of some permanence, nor the authority of constituting a discipline, requiring talent and training. Knowledge becomes a servant of the individual or the group's pathos: its truth is a function of how effectively it releases. Within the field of public administration, including the industrial state, this means positivism. But knowledge detached from salvational goals has weak credentials. When its sole function is to enable psychological remission it is always in danger of losing credibility - through failing to relieve. Alternatively, when its sole function is positivistically remissive, it is also in danger of collapsing - this time because the remissive culture's technocrats will inevitably tire of believing the objectivist illusions on which their work servicing the service industries is predicated. Remissive knowledge, in both of its forms, is on the threshold of epistemological nihilism.

Puritan knowledge was either positivist, in the service of objective truth, or subjectivist, serving ethos, revealing its parameters. In both cases thought contained in part its own goal; it was not an utterly utilitarian instrument. Even Nietzsche and Husserl pursued *self*-understanding: for them there was an existent, and it was to be understood. In the remissive culture, however, knowledge is reduced to an aspect of technology, cosseting, servicing and entertaining.

The remissive thus means the end of ideology. Like positivism it has no place for morally-charged systems of belief. Nietzsche's 'beyond good and evil' comes finally to realization, as he feared, in the alternative forms of instrumentally positivist knowledge and epistemological nihilism. Idealism, if it too does not lapse with the decline of authoritative knowledge, will be remissively channelled, either publicly into social work, or privately into the visionary pursuit of subjective fantasy.

Deteriorating confidence in the substantiality of knowledge in the human sciences has been matched by a parallel change within the institutions that transmit knowledge from one generation to the next. Universities have gained an increasingly important place in modern societies: the identification with the medieval church has some cogency in that it is more and more the organs of highest learning that provide the wider community with symbols, information and guidance. This greater centrality has been reinforced in the last decade by the phenomenon of students forming the vanguard of political dissidence.

The same political restiveness has led students to force radical transformations of the rituals of the class-room. Traditional structures of pedagogical authority have been eroded. The place of the dedicated specialist scholar becomes marginal within the university; he is more regarded as an anachronism. The teacher is no longer a distant, aloof, magisterial figure, the Herr Doktor Professor of German academia. While there is still room for charismatic presence, it is less reinforced by the dignity of office. Moreover, the best students have fewer resources for concentration; they are more likely than in previous decades to *drop-out*. The passion for knowledge is rare; even rarer is the person with a true calling for learning.

Some of the dynamics of this transition are not new. In part it may be seen as yet another practical working through of the law that Tocqueville drew from his nineteenth-century observations of America, that under democracy the majority is much better educated, but the high quality of education that had been available to the élite few in an aristocratic culture is lost.

The remissive has nowhere been as successfully implemented as within the universities. The Puritan emphasis on discipline within the narrow specialist confines of a man's calling has given way to a more polymorphous and dilettantish style of enquiry, and repeated demands for relevancy - which means remissive relevancy, for knowledge that might enhance the student's sense of ease. A teacher finds it progressively more difficult to pursue single themes thoroughly: to attract students he needs the skills of the mass entertainer, to stimulate his audience with histrionic promises of novelty. What started in part as a salutary revulsion at the triviality of positivist-conceived hypotheses has gained momentum as a rejection of that inner discipline indispensable to true learning. The commendable pursuit of personally or socially relevant knowledge has proved, within the cosseting walks of the modern university, all too readily to degenerate into the pursuit of titillation and distraction - that is, entertainment.

The university in recent decades has, moreover, become, for many of that increasing proportion of students who choose humanities, the venue where neither qualifications to enter élite vocations are won nor learning sought; it has become rather an institution combining the functions of the luxury hotel and the hospital, a sanctuary for a few years from a public reality whose purposes do not compel. But the university as sanatorium becomes less and less the peculiar asylum for the talented and sane young, and more the exemplary institution in a remissive-hedonist culture, constitutive of a public reality in which disciplined work gradually makes way for desultory play.

Western culture has been predicated on the master-apprentice model of transmitting learning and skill. Whether individual authority was borne by the master craftsman, the professor or the priest/preacher, the apprentice-student-layman knew the rigours of the role he must play if one day he was to be worthy of mastership. The relationship of father to son was endowed with a similar symbolic. Now the confidence of the teachers and fathers is weak: they are not sure themselves of the value of their traditional task of administering and communicating the culture they dutifully inherited. Fathers now turn to their own sons for guidance, a phenomenon Plato knew, and identified with the roots of disorder, the decline of a binding sense of law over and above individual desire. In such a condition of permanent cultural revolution, or anarchy, the only alternative to nihilism is to make a norm of undermining all norms, a norm that well complements the remissive-hedonist's repressed consciousness of his own moralism.

Thus the popularity of sociology, the intellectual retreat of those ethically homeless who retain relativizing enthusiasms, and in particular the popularity of its latest fashion, 'ethnomethodology', California's contribution to epistemological nihilism. But a normative war on norms cannot endure: once the last attachments to the old values are broken so is the passion for resistance, and the exercise loses its sense. In the past, in theory and in practice, new norms would have replaced old; today, however, we move ideologically towards the all-pervading normless norm of welfare. But if we ever arrive in practice we shall find bland nihilist opacity rather than the garden of earthly delights.

But the most serious disjunction between remissive personality and ideology is over *work*. Remissive-hedonist ideology returns to the pre-Puritan view that work is drudgery, to be avoided at all costs; on the other hand, *play* is of the human essence. Perhaps there was a time when men were psychologically capable of carefree play, a true epoch of hedonism. However, what we know about the human instincts, about guilt and about the constraining imperative of culture, suggests that such an arcadia was always a utopian hope sought to ameliorate the alternative fact, that deep play, desperately serious, ritualized, endlessly repeated with each return of the repressed, is universal to human conduct (and certainly to Western conduct).

Whatever the ultimate truth about the links between Calvinism and capitalism, one of the necessary conditions for the development of the latter was the introduction, through the infusing of this-worldly activity with the pursuit of other-worldly ends, of a new attitude to work. Irrational work was the engine of capitalism. Concurrently, play too was redefined. With the instating of the Puritan notion of vocation, work and play became mutually dependent. Thereafter men would find their play absorbing only when it contained a religious element, when it was deeply serious in both providing expression for inner truths and pointing beyond itself. Their play became both catharsis and a means of redemption, and thus identical with work, and, more specifically, with vocation. Romanticism emerged from this same tradition to idealize 'art' as the unique synthesis: art for the Romantic was passionate vocation, its object intensely personal, its end, in one guise or another, salvational.

The West remains psychologically heir to this view of the

complementarity of work and play. Its children who seek play that is not at the same time work consequently find that their ideals lead them into a reality of depressive boredom. A philosophy of leisure is culturally irrelevant, except as ideological compensation for failing Puritans who cannot discover a vocation. Hobbies and pastimes are not deeply serious; that is they are not harnessed to other-worldly ends. Not bearing grace or charisma, they cannot absorb for long; their presence does not echo. One of the remissive's aims in his war against inherited guilt is to divorce play from work. What he in fact achieves is the erosion of the play/work dialectic and its replacement by the perpetual distraction of entertainment, which is ultimately boring. Here is the operative antithesis.

Reinhard Bendix details in his book, *Work and Authority in Industry*, a major change in the ideology of work in Britain and the USA this century. The old, nineteenth-century view celebrated individual character and effort, it employed images of the struggle for survival, and of the dominant motive of self-interest, images which worked in harmony with national interest; authority was based on success and a self-evident sense of superiority; the entrepreneur himself stood as exemplar for the conduct of all men. Bendix focuses on the 1920s and 1930s as the period of decisive transition in the USA. A new ideology emerged that emphasized individual adaptability rather than character, the virtue of co-operative teamwork rather than that of egoistic competition. The power of the manager declined as experts, ranging from industrial psychologists to management consultants, gained influence; the managerial task shifted from moral exhortation to scientific planning, the skilful organization of co-operative effort.

Let us consider one business situation, that of company failure. It has become less the manager as an individual who is responsible and more the tools available to him. Such failure, for example in the modulation of expertise, or in the flow of information, promotes a search for new and better knowledge, rather than for a new and better manager. Alternatively, the total system is seen to be at fault, the company a victim of economic forces beyond its control. As the individual loses power and responsibility, as his forming hand - what the classical Romans called his *virtus* - becomes enfeebled, he is moved to resign himself to the play of larger forces, to see himself as a small cog in the great system of *fortuna*.

The ideology of work necessarily changed also for the employee.

The ethic of hard work gave way to that of mateship, of successful human relations. Whereas the worker who was previously merely an inferior cog in the factory machine may have now become a happier cog (as some sociologists have speculated), the worker who had formerly had a vocation now found his work devalued into a means for remissive pleasure, in the form of camaraderie at work, and consumption at home. In either case the transition was remissive, in the former case for the better, in the latter for the worse.

The notion of the remissive contains obvious implications about the changing role of authority in the domain of the erotic. To focus exclusively on pleasure as the goal, to become reluctant to postpone gratification, is to start proceedings for the divorce of love from sex. Sex is animalist pleasure; love is one of the means fantasizing men have chosen to endow a basically physical activity with metaphysical dimensions - in this case spiritual dignity, and therefore authority. No human eroticism is purely animalist - that is, unpermeated by fantasy - although intellect may play a 'perverting' rather than spiritualizing or ennobling role. The remissive trend is to demythologize eros, to reduce its status to that of one of many sensual pleasures, available as and when desired, without obligations.

The West's erotic inheritance passes down from the most highly sublimated extreme, that of Romantic love, predicated on the related prohibitions of chastity and fidelity, displaying the central psychological motif of indefinitely postponed gratification. Although the monogamous marriage, the institutionalized form of the Romantic myth, was not general until the nineteenth century, the notion of ascetic love had infused the manners and mores of various social élites since the early middle ages. The counter-process of loosening the bonds of sublimation has gained momentum only this century, after much resistance from, amongst others, the Puritan, the Rousseauist Romantic and, in selective ways, the bourgeois. The authority of Romantic passion, of its guiding fantasy, has been worn down by a long tearing at its ethical halters, in turn chastity and fidelity. As yet the West is too Puritan for the authority of love to have been dispelled in any comprehensive sense. Indeed, there may be a psychological law that the higher the price in instinctual renunciation that has been paid for a cultural gain - in this case Romantic love and its many secular manifestations - the longer the period of deconversion.

One social manifestation of the pressure for erotic revaluation has been the revival at an unprecedented pitch of movements for female emancipation. In spite of the paranoid political style prevalent in these movements, they represent a symptom of the emergence of the remissive. The hallmark of a patriarchal society has been strong controls administered by means of stern individual authority. The success of women's protest indicates the widespread acceptance of its first claim, that the patriarchal ordering principle is now obsolete. One of the leading counter-images is of a female politics, more personal and sensitive, governed by the method of the forgiving mother rather than the forbidding father. The symbols are Catholic, to the point of isolating the Puritan and the patriarchal as the marks of the devil.

As *leitmotif* to these transitions in erotic style appears the growing rarity of masculine males strongly attracted to women, a corresponding development of masculine traits in women, and a proliferation of homosexual explorations amongst both sexes. The pattern is as yet too elusive to interpret confidently; what, however, may be said is that the decline of Puritan authority, which was patriarchal, is being mirrored in the changing patterns of comparative erotic disposition of men and women.

Here in the erotic, as elsewhere, the changes that are actually occurring are misrepresented by remissive ideology. Lapsing Puritans groping for a hedonist ideal forget the genre of true sensuality available to them by virtue of their origins. Sensuality as we know it is deeply infused and sustained by a Puritan temper. That complex logic of guarded approach, timid withdrawal, tentative return, acute sensitivity to changes in distance, indeed a need to play out the lessening of distance in elaborate rituals, play that both articulates passion and by postponing gratification intensifies it, the diffusing of this intensity into a charged symbolic incorporating landscape, scents, details of gesture, mien, fall of the hair in the erotic drama, a diffusion that at the same time by releasing new dimensions of imagination serves to further intensify the experience - all this is dependent upon a Puritan *pudeur* towards the private, and a Puritan faith that what is ultimately at stake is not the game to surpass all games but, in some sense, salvation. In this symbolic, love has authority.

The remissive's hedonism is a utopia special to failing Puritans, and is founded on delusion. Only a Westerner such as D. H.

Lawrence with his outlets for passion chronically distorted by a
malign Puritanism could so project a private fantasy of utopia as to
find in the image of the bull, and his prosaic sexual discharge, a
model for human gratification. Again the sins of the fathers have
proved insidiously binding, by permitting the son to conceive only
of a delusional course of remission. Lawrence was just one of many
Western intellectuals, who, falling victim to the asceticism integral
to his calling, reacted to the split he saw in himself between mind
and   body,   at   the   latter's   expense,   by   a   compensatory
over-estimation of body's potential. (Hence his prominence as
moral guide in the Victorian corners of even contemporary
university English departments.)

Indeed, this modern version of the hedonist ideal is a specifically
Puritan product, symptom of the tradition in decline, when all that
was best in it is lost and only its pathology survives. Pure hedonism
as an ideal will turn out in practice to be physical rather than
sensual, stupefying rather than intoxicating.

The sexual hedonism of the remitted man is decadent. A culture
in which shops merchandising accessory gadgets flourish, in which
planned inebriation on tequila or hashish is prerequisite for sexual
interest, in which students can phlegmatically relate their servicing
of four bedrooms in one night, is one which is inwardly dead.
Culture in Simmel's sense is vestigial where there is nothing left of
that Puritan experience of shy erotic play only through whose
self-absorbing prolongation is the precarious achievement of trust
and affection established. (It was the seventeenth-century English
Puritans who stressed friendship between man and wife, a working
partnership based on private intimacy and public competence.)
Where there is no inner man to be mediated there can be no call for
those cultural values, including language itself, by means of which
men sought to articulate and make intelligible and trustworthy that
invisibly traced disposition of being, striving for form, which was,
somehow, their essence.

The remissive-hedonist's mode is orally-indulgent here as
elsewhere. It places relationship as a means of consumption, and is
victim of the consumer's psychological constraint of diminishing
marginal returns in pleasure, which can be compensated for only by
novelty ploys. The remissive was deceived by a false analogy when he
set about reducing the erotic from its position of peculiar
psychological centrality in the Western tradition to a status equal to

food. His guiding image was that of the feast. He believed that feasts could provide him with endless pleasure. But they do so only for gourmets, and the remissive is not a gourmet. To be a gourmet requires passion; it is a calling; it depends on the Puritan attachment to standards of excellence. The remissive quickly tires of feasting, unless he rations himself, which requires him to act against his nature. Even when he manages to set up a range of sensual delights, including erotic games, his capacity for sustaining them is not strong: they have no authority over him.

Karl Mannheim, in the last of his *Essays on the Sociology of Culture*, selects the rise of democracy as the leading theme in European social history over the last half millennium. He defines democratization sociologically rather than politically, as the process of transformation from aristocratic to egalitarian orders through the progressive elimination of social distance. His interpretation has many parallels with what has been conceptualized here as the decline of individual authority.

But the break-down of social distance over this period has been balanced by a correlative distancing of man from nature, and from the most 'natural' of human associations, the community. In the schema employed here this is the displacement of individual authority into the institutional, notably undemocratic, leviathan of the public sphere. Remissive-hedonist man seeks to restore some of the intimate patterns of community, while valuing the distance inherent in the anonymity and mobility forced upon him by technocratic living. (That the distance, in whatever form, at which man lives from his fellow man is psychologically indispensable to him, is at the core of his sense of unredeemable original sin.)

The remissive is in search of space, which he believes he will gain once he has collapsed distance. But it is precisely the distance between an individual's instincts and his significant objects, that is, the range over which he projects his wishes, that gives him room in which to work. When the distance between nerve and act contracts to zero, neurosis becomes claustrophobic, rigid; it cannot be played out. The winning of trust, of intimacy (one of the marks of sanity, the other being vocation), is a coming closer, and requires initial distance, and thereafter the repeated discipline of attaining distance in order to conquer it anew.

Mannheim points out that a democratic culture emphasizes

function and process rather than Gestalt. It dismisses as ameliorably repressive whatever is fixed or determined - form, structure, ethos. But its optimism about the malleability of things is considerably deluded. We have known, certainly since Mosca and Michels, that the large-scale institutions of the modern capitalist state impose an iron law of oligarchy; through time they have progressively reduced possibilities for democratic control within the public world. The modern democrat is left with a small public arena in which to operate realistically. On the other hand, in the private domain, his humanist tolerance of his fellow man is winning out over the Puritan attachment to character. (Mannheim's categories apply imperfectly here, as it was a distance different from the social one of mediaeval aristocracy that Puritanism sought to establish.)

The great theorist of democracy, and anticipator of the remissive, remains Tocqueville. He wrote of 'men living in democratic ages':

> Forms excite their contempt and often their hatred; as they
> commonly aspire to none but easy and present gratifications,
> they rush onwards to the object of their desires, and the slightest
> delay exasperates them. This same temper, carried with them
> into political life, renders them hostile to forms, which
> perpetually retard or arrest them in some of their projects.

Form, structure, ethos - all depend on, and in turn reinforce, authority. At the opposite pole, flux, anarchy, nihilism, pathos are inherently egalitarian. The process of democratization continues today psychologically, in the individual's pursuit of living minute by minute, grasping each new fancy as it occurs, absorbed in acting out a series of random associations. The paradigm is the child with a box of toys, seizing the first one that catches his eye, playing with it until his attention starts to wander and he spots another. Curiosity is never sustained. The laws of hedonism put novelty at a premium. The day, the year, the lifetime has no basic pattern, no form. Time, however it is delimited, is registered as a series of games, all offering their own individual pleasures, none pointing beyond themselves or echoing a deeper meaning. I shall return in the next chapter, on paranoia, to consider the democrat's hostility to political forms.

Social literature has made much of the trend, which has heightened in the last decade, of individuals seeking greater personal autonomy. Stress has been placed on 'self-realization' and 'self-awareness', in particular in the domains of education and psychotherapy, with the intention of nourishing what has been alluded to as a stronger sense of inner authority. I have already suggested in relation to psychotherapy that interest in the authority of self is historically transient and pre-remissive. The remissive culture harbours no preferred character types, so it has no need for exemplars - every man does his own thing in his own way. The term 'authority' is obsolete, for no one requires commandments. In a culture in which constraints are weakened there will automatically be more autonomy than hitherto. But the individual emerges as an autonomous pleasure-seeker, a free-floating entity of impulse, a particle in an ocean of forces, like Camus's Meursaut, rather than a personality. 'Experience' becomes a range of sensations, not a means for learning. Inner authority depends on commitment to a constraining structure of self, and in turn the primacy of ethos; but, for remissive-hedonist man, ego in this sense finally reveals itself as a cage, serving no purpose but to limit his pleasures.

The remissive 'new education', whose presiding norm is that the child's every wish be immediately satisfied, succeeds in nurturing inner authority only in the cases of children who bring with them Puritan natures. Then a teacher who works at neutralizing socially-reinforced guilts and pointing out new imaginative horizons may lessen the likelihood of the child being cripplingly inhibited. But even with Puritan types it is foolhardy to prescribe paths of character formation.

The progressive disenchantment of work has been mirrored in a parallel process in education. We can readily distinguish four historical stages. The Calvinist who worked for God sought knowledge of that same God; he educated himself so as to be able to interpret the scriptures. The second stage to develop was that of work for its own sake, of vocation, still harnessed to salvational hopes, but secularized, no longer perceived in theological symbols. This stage in the evolution of the concept of work had its equivalent in knowledge for its own sake, a pursuit drawn by the transcendental goal of truth. The pursuit of knowledge for its own sake has lain behind most of the finer achievements of Western intellectual culture. The third stage to develop was that of utilitarian work, work as a means to a purely materialist end. It had its parallel in education as training for a career. (My suspicion, however, is that this form of work rarely if ever existed as such, that it too drew its energy from strivings after immortality.) Finally, with the remissive, and the

attempt to replace work by play, education too loses its traditional
purposes, which are replaced by the hedonist ideology of the child
doing what he likes, what takes his fancy.

Education plays a crucial role in the decline of individual
authority. The new education is to be remissive, the means for
escaping from the Puritan past; it is hostile to inherited culture, and
its own traditional function of transmitting that culture and its
commitments; it is hostile even to its standard function of
providing a training in citizenship, or at the most elementary level,
in social competence, for it rejects the measures of that competence.
The remissive trend surfaces in the slackening of the syllabus, the
steady elimination of language requirements for higher education
(on grounds of relevance), the introduction of open classes in which
lessons are not structured, in which the intention is that the child
decides what he will do, how he will do it and for how long. The real
consequences of this 'de-schooling' have been submerged under an
incoming tide of ideology.

I wish to examine some of the consequences. First, there will in
the future, as in the past, inevitably be a few charismatic teachers,
and they may benefit from a slackening of external commands.
Indeed, their style of teaching by inspiration, to children who are
moved to work with passion, and who therefore find education a
pleasure, has itself contributed to the remissive ideal of an
education grounded in emotion rather than in authority. But again
this is a disastrous misreading. Charisma is authority of the most
potent kind; the children's playful pleasure is a product of the
security they feel in the presence of a true father, coddled by his
guiding protection. This situation, rather than presenting some
embodiment of the democratic ideal, represents precisely its
opposite: the distance between the charismatic and his flock, in
spite of the apparent intimacy, is vast and irreducible, the very
reason that he does not need the support of institutions, or
intermediaries, to bolster his authority. The analogous relationship
is that of Calvinism's elect to non-elect, separated by an intractable
distance; the literal Greek meaning of 'charismatic' was 'carrying
God's grace'.

Slack structures suit charismatics and no one else. For the rest they
let loose confusion and anomie, and therefore depression. Again
remission provides an ideology, *faute de mieux*. Teachers,
education departments, communities who have been shaken by

anti-Puritan ideology rationalize in remissive terms their utter bewilderment about what education ought to be. Letting the child have his own head is a way out for a teacher (or parent) who has no idea of what to do with him - no idea, that is, of what it means to be a teacher, no sense of the responsibility of that vocation. It is a culturally and socially suicidal error for fathers who have lost the will to command to assume that children are inwardly purposive and will, without guidance, mature as sane citizens and leaders. Inertia is all that can come out of this inversion of the biologically, psychologically and socially indispensable relation of father/teacher to dependant/child. 'Self-realization' becomes the rationalization of chaos. The parent or teacher who is unable to say 'No!' communicates not the ease of freedom, but anomic panic, generative of both delinquency and depression. Symptomatic of current moral paralysis is the displacement of reformist zeal into the bureaucratic surrogates of providing more money for buildings, and allowing teachers and their unions to capitalize on the lapse of command by moving for higher salaries and better physical conditions. The irony of the remissive cultural revolution is that it has facilitated the routinization of education.

Finally, remissive education in practice serves to maintain social inequalities, in spite of the levelling ideology of its bourgeois advocates. The children of literate, cultured families can survive the open class-room without decisive handicap from its failure to educate in the crucial cumulative skills of being able to read, write, count and interpret the world. Some may in fact benefit, as true Puritans, from its freedom from routine pedagogy. But for that majority which comes from homes where there is little incentive for analytical play, a school that does not painstakingly compensate, by teaching the skills basic to becoming a competent citizen, reduces chances of social mobility. Migrant children, in Australia for example, from families whose English is poor, constitute only the most obvious extreme of the majority whose principal need from schools is for simple, practical education, and for whom 'doing your own thing' is gibberish and fatal to their pre-remissive aspirations. (A society is always a maze of parallel paths: compare here the insensitive hypocrisy of those many highly-educated feminists, unhappy in their own lonely independence from marriage, who preach that the nuclear family is degrading for *all* women.)

The characteristically remissive call for closer integration of school and community may well louden. But the attaching of the anomic school to the hardly less anomic community has little chance of fortifying either. Those who are working for the egalitarian elimination of ethos, the elimination of discipline from schooling, under the correct assumption that discipline and training generate distance, are in fact bringing about the demoralization of education, their activity masquerading under a communalistic ethic. But even if the community falls for the ideology and stops caring whether its children are learned, it is unlikely to approve of the school relinquishing its child-minding function; nor are parents likely to agree to participate voluntarily themselves, as lay educators, in the schools.

The demoralization of education illustrates the general law that attempts to do away with hierarchy, to open all doors and knock down all walls, whether driven by egalitarian ideals or not, favour the few, those who are confident and relatively autonomous, while removing the supports that enable the many to live with some dignity and purpose. The virtue of forms, as the great political philosophers have taught, is that they protect the many from their own unruly impulses and from the corruption and tyranny that their inwardly remiss natures unwittingly foster. Forms rarely constrain the able; indeed, it is the democratic-remissive hostility to position and distinction that is more likely to inhibit ability. To abolish social distance means to instate an anarchy in which only the fittest, that is the few, will survive in any worthwhile sense. Thus the way is prepared to the greatest and most intractable distance of all, that between the chosen and the unchosen. Social anarchy, nevertheless, is rarely beneficial even for the few, although they may survive it better. In most cases they too depend on a milieu that is stable, and that additionally is discriminating enough to appreciate their work. The old, worldly, post-utopian Plato came to the view that reason is only for the few, magic for the many. We are today experiencing the consequences of Benda's *trahison des clercs*, as those who rightfully should have constituted the few look to the many, and their opinion, for reason, and themselves take up magic. How much of today's most potent magic, remissive ideology itself, in its many guises, has originated in the universities, from where it has spread through the mass media, through schools, business, government. The modern university is the single institution that had the influence and the resources to work against the remissive, to reinforce the authority of old cultural forms and to create legitimacy for new ones. In fact it has worked precisely in the opposite direction. It ought to take much of the responsibility for the successful evolution of remissive culture. I leave until the next chapter, on paranoia, further discussion of the magic that has been sought by those whose role it should have been to champion reason.

I am not, of course, arguing that all constraints are warranted. When old forms lose their vitality, and turn into desiccated husks, there can be no argument for retaining them. My concern has been solely with the general trend of rising hostility to authority as such, of blanket approval of anything that might be described as a gain in autonomy. But even within this trend qualifications should be made. For instance, there has been a tradition since Freud that, while not wholly pursuing a remissive-hedonist ideology, has dedicated itself to minimizing the degree to which social definitions of marriage, sex, child-rearing and so on govern human relationships. Its representatives, such as K. Perutz (*Marriage is Hell*, 1972), are usually disguised Puritans, who, like their seventeenth-century forebears, protest at the intrusion of community norms into the essentially private endeavour of creating this-worldly links with salvation. The Puritan ideal of marriage, man and wife in co-operative friendship, and the Puritan emphasis on vigilant work and relentless rational application as prerequisite for fulfilment, find renewed presence in this contemporary striving for autonomy, responsibility and constant sensitivity to each individual's needs and to the unforeseen turnings in the unforeseeable path of character's living with character. This tradition, by virtue of its construction of a hybrid Puritan-remissive ideology, accepts the Puritan disposition of its adherents.

A democratic culture affirms change. It is optimistic, in the tradition of rationalist humanism; its imagination is directed towards creating a better future. Its ontological paradigm may be read in Sartre's existentialist proclamations, taken to an extreme in the 1946 formulation: 'Man is free and there is no human nature which I can take as foundational.' The aristocrat, like the Puritan, was more conservative, interested in history and in origins: character depended on slow maturing under favourable conditions from strong foundations. Thus the élitist fatalism, and the attendant

authority of the past, are both anathema to the democrat. Part of
the remissive's moralism is his hostility to the past: his ideology
centres on liberation from evil origins.

It has proved economically efficacious to abolish the past. The
industrial state is tooled up to service a culture that operates
according to a first principle of rapid change. And remissive man
prefers it so: without change in his environment, in his
commodities, in his acquaintances, he is quickly bored. For him the
past is a world in which pleasures, serviced by another technology,
enjoyed at another tempo, were qualitatively different; as such it is
of no immediate interest.

Disregard for the past has been directly complemented by waning
respect for what was traditionally called wisdom - an understanding
of life gained from long and varied experience. The Western notion
of wisdom depended on a guiding attachment to character and its
formation, to *Bildung*, to the unfolding and consolidating, over
many years, of personality. Personality was conceived of as the
foundation structure for the emotional vicissitudes that made of
wisdom a vital integrating and sustaining force. By contrast, the
contemporary interest in occult and oriental wisdom bears the
characteristics of a remissive fad: treating wisdom as a commodity,
instantly accessible, the more obscure its origins the more engaging
its novelty, it employs it as a technique for enriching the sensory
kaleidoscope, and symbolically distancing itself from the old
culture. This is precisely the mark of a culture that has no respect for
the past, and no understanding of the wisdom of seers.

The demise of the traditional sage ethic has also meant that,
during the paranoid stage of transition, the aged have been turned
into human refuse. Remissive society has not as yet provided for
them - their plight has proved to be of low priority. Meanwhile they
are stranded, morally and socially destitute, stripped of their
traditional dignity, that of being the bearers and transmitters of the
culture's highest truths. Their role as the carriers of wisdom was
played out in such activities as telling tales that would be
absorbingly relevant to the young as sources of information, as
morals laudatory of heroic traits and as contacts with a past that was
suffused with significance. Without traditions and churches, elders
are redundant; without character, exemplars are redundant. To
focus on the future and on change renders all that is 'old'
redundant. A hedonist golden age depends not only on no one

asking for other than pleasure: to avoid producing human waste, its institutional structure must be able to service *all* needs, including those of the aged.

A discussion of the changing patterns in attitudes to the importance of traditions, of binding forms and mapping structures, must turn finally to a consideration of art. Twentieth-century art (painting, sculpture, music, literature) has been widely discussed as constituting a break in the Western tradition, a rejection of the principles on which Western art has been traditionally predicated. To enter this discussion is to plunge into a pricklebush; merely to begin with any sensitivity would require a lengthy examination of the intricate problem of the role of form in art. My intention is to flank and make some comments in passing on leading themes that exhibit affinities with the remissive.

The first theme is of increasing subjectivism. The development since the late eighteenth century of subjectivist epistemology has been paralleled by a similar movement in literature. The line runs from the early Romantics and their concern with self, with inwardness, with feeling, impulse and sensation, through the *Bildungsroman* to modern, post-1890 literature, influenced by Nietzsche and later Freud, devoted to exploring the most subjective world of all, that of the unconscious and its multiple sedimentations in private consciousness - the literature of Joyce, Proust, Virginia Woolf, Rilke, of Kafka, Camus and Beckett. In painting, the expressionist and surrealist movements attempted a similar rendering of the isolated world of the subjective and usually tormented consciousness. The development of subjectivism, as already discussed earlier in this essay in the case of epistemology, eliminates one of the bulwarks against nihilism by reinforcing the individual's distance from his community, weakening his commitment to its purposes and reducing the scope of his absorptions to those of private fantasy. Those very witty and exuberantly inventive subjectivists, the Dadaists, defined themselves by making fun of the ways of the public social order of their day.

The second theme is of increasing amoralism. Traditionally Western art has been moral, devoted to revealing and affirming the culture's central beliefs and guiding symbolic. This was as true for the medieval painter glorifying themes from the Gospels as it was for Donatello's sculpture, Bach's church music and Tolstoy's novels. Even in the nineteenth century, when culture's heterogeneity had become more apparent, art in the main preserved its commitment to ethos, devoting itself to one or another of the symbolic universes of the time. But the emergence of what may be précised as the 'art for art's sake' movement forced a radical change. The new impulse was to divest art of its moral content, remove its messages and abstract it from the passions of its creator, leaving him free to concentrate on form, on style. There were antecedents. Raphael, for instance, may have been as interested in achieving perfect forms, deriving from classical geometry, as illustrating morals. But Flaubert and his heirs went much farther than simply recognizing a craftsman's pleasure in technical success. Flaubert wrote:

> What seems beautiful to me, what I should like to write, is a book about nothing, a book dependent on nothing external, which would be held together by the strength of its style, just as the earth, suspended in the void, depends on nothing external for its support; a book which would have almost no subject, or at least in which the subject would be almost invisible, if such a thing is possible. The finest works of art are those that contain the least matter; . . . The less one feels a thing, the more fit one is to express it in its true nature.

Mallarmé insisted that the 'enthusiastic' poet disappear from the finished poem. Wilde quipped: 'There is no such thing as a moral or an immoral book. Books are well written, or badly written.' Cézanne stressed that the art object is autonomous, governed by its own laws. (I take these views more as illustrations of the emerging theory of art than as convincing interpretations of what Flaubert, for instance, actually did in his own novels.)

The theme of growing amoralism in art has various branches in the twentieth century. One branch moves through painting that is purely abstract, in the sense of non-representational of human situations - the painting of Klee, Mondrian, Pollock and a plethora of others. Another branch consists of works that continue to portray human beings, but show them depersonalized, divested of their moral content, operating more like machines than psyches. Belonging here are some of the works of the *nouveau roman*, of surrealist painting and poetry, of Beckett. At the end of one branch of the detachment of art from morals is technological sculpture, in which intricate, automated apparatuses employing mirrors, lights, rotating bars and plates, have transformed technical gimmickry into a fantastic visual kaleidoscope.

Amoral art is one step closer to nihilism than was subjectivist art. At its best it has not relaxed its commitment to forms; indeed no one has been more dedicated to the perfect form than Flaubert, with his description of art as a 'long patience'. Yet it has broken completely with its traditional interdictory function. Amoral art belongs to the remissive in its indifference to moral bonds, in its not wishing to contaminate itself with the affairs of the hearth, the market place or the parliament. It has served as a major influence in one of the contemporary degradations of art into entertainment, in ephemeral works employing optical illusions, neon lights, simulated technology.

The third and final theme is of lessening respect for forms. Modern art has defined itself by its ambition to break free from the constraints of old forms. But if it is to be distinguished from earlier periods of innovation, which necessarily had also to overturn inherited taste and technique, then the argument must demonstrate a trend of lessening respect for form in itself. This is no simple matter, for it remains true today that the finest art exhibits high technical competence. I wish here solely to note some of the attempts to do away with form altogether. In painting there have been moves to break out of the picture frame, to abandon brushes. Erich Kahler writes, in his *The Disintegration of Form in the Arts*, of the ubiquitous hold of the *avant-garde* movement:

> Under the fanfares of thrilling innovations sounding everywhere, from Brazil to Iceland, literature fades away, not only into graphics, but into motley sound associations and mechanistic regimentation. There are 'pop poems', 'audio poems', 'machine poems', 'concrete', 'visual', and 'phonic' poetry. Henri Chopin's 'audiopoem' is a flux of natural and mechanical sounds (spoken and recorded by the poet) ranging from breathings, grunts, clicks, and whistles, to dentist's drills, circular saws, ship's horns, and distant planes.

John Cage, in the vanguard of contemporary music, has written:

> [Composers should] give up the desire to control sound, clear
> [their] mind of music and set about discovering means to let
> sounds be themselves rather than vehicles for man-made theories
> or expressions of human sentiments. . . .
>
> In *Music for Piano*, and subsequent pieces, indeed, structure is
> no longer a part of composition means. The view taken is not of
> an activity the purpose of which is to integrate the opposites, but
> rather of an activity characterized by process and essentially
> purposeless. The mind, though stripped of its right to control, is
> still present. . . . I derived the method I use for writing music by
> tossing coins from the method used in the *Book of Changes* for
> obtaining oracles.

The focus here on randomness directly contravenes the classical
principles of Western art, which held that no element in a work
could be arbitrary, no relationship imprecise. However, one
generalizes at risk, for the analogous development in physics led to
the establishment of a new theoretical perspective, a new order of
forms (I refer to the development through which the fixed order of
Newtonian mechanics, founded on the assumption that
determinate objects move along determined paths, was progressively eroded into the relativist, indeterminate world of quantum
mechanics).

Whether or not a new tradition will grow out of electronic music,
as Cage and McLuhan have intimated, there are remissive traits in
this music's utilization of everyday sounds, in its ambition to
incorporate 'spontaneously' any unprogrammed noises, in its
hostility to the past, in its preference for the random, the
disconnected, the discordant, the ephemeral, and finally in its aim
to close the gap between art and experience, making art immediate
rather than a mediator. This art provides a metaphor for the
remissive ideal of the individual free from disposition, free to choose
his experiences as if by the spin of a roulette wheel; in this art the
remissive ideal appears to be realized. To vary the example, a new
genre within the most *avant-garde* of all media, the movie film, also
succeeds in serving the remissive's ludic style: the technique is to
bombard the senses with a rapid sequence of random images,
colours and sounds. The so-called 'underground' introduced these
Gestalt-free films; by now advertisers have recognized their

potential for capitivating the contemporary audience.

Far along the subjectivist line, and in opposition to Flaubert's credo, Mark Rothko has asserted that 'a painting is not a picture of an experience; it is an experience'. Art as experience, as event, as happening, is purely of the remissive and likely to be remiss in form. Of this genre is the primitivist, anti-intellectual poetry of Ginsberg, who has proclaimed: 'Unscrew the locks from the doors! Unscrew the doors from their jambs!' Here ideology complements lack of concern with technical excellence.

Behind the rare exceptions traditions of excellence are under stress. For example, reports of art schools in the USA indicate that the mania for novelty has produced fashions that change at such a bewildering rate that teaching, as instruction in technique and the passing on of traditional discriminations, has been rendered impossible. Each new vogue brings with it a new discipline. The critic Harold Rosenberg writes in his book, *The De-definition of Art*:

> Beyond the quality of the teacher, there is the problem that art changes almost from season to season in outlook, concept, and even the materials out of which it is made. If the subject being taught could be defined, the matter of whether those who teach it are first-rate or second-rate might be less important. As it is, even the quality of an artist's work is beyond dispute, an attempt by him to encompass each new move in the art world makes him, as a teacher, in effect second-rate, since only the inventor of the new move is first-rate in relation to it. . . . Ambitious students are apt to be aware of this situation; no matter how distinguished the creations of their artist-teacher, they regard him as inadequate to impart the latest mode popular in New York. Speaking to a university audience, Jack Tworkov, then Chairman of the Art Department at Yale, observed that students in his department . . . scarcely listened to their teachers but derived their ideas from art journals.

Encompassing these themes, looming as their common offspring, is the decline of art into entertainment. The experience of beauty must be distinguished from that of entertainment. Beauty exhilarates; in its intimation of some eternal harmony, some image of perfection, some mysterious and enduring truth, it brings a serene and compelling joy. Beauty mediates reality, it reveals deepest essences; in Heidegger's words it is what tears us out of the oblivion of being, and gives us a view of that being. Moreover, its images endure; it is not transitory. This holds for the amoral art of Cézanne or Klee as much as it does for the overtly moral works of Milton. (Art that is amoral of the *first* order, that is non-representational of human situations, may be moral of the *second* order. This occurs when it achieves harmony of form, some quintessential balance or proportion of line, colour or sound. Second-order morality is not associated with specific human acts, but is cosmic, praising the perfection and mystery of nature, of the universe, of a grand design of which man is but one tiny element. It inspires man with the glory of that design, connecting him to it.)

The pursuit of beauty, and in particular the quest for an image of perfection, bears the lineaments of Puritanism, in the broad psychological terms in which it has been interpreted in this essay. Entertainment, by contrast, serves entirely as a means of release; rather than mediating reality or truth it provides an escape from their onerous necessity. Entertainment distracts. (Distraction is a Puritan notion; it is born of the assumption that there is some central 'traction'.) Entertainment, serving as a means of detachment from structured reality or ethos of any form, is at the core of the remissive culture's affairs. From the ideological standpoint in a fully-fledged remissive culture, moreover, there is no reality or truth, bearing traces of the absolute, which art as traditionally conceived could mediate. Beauty is redefined as successful expression, without reference to tradition: the aesthetics of 'doing your own thing'.

The argument is not meant to imply that men are nobler when they live without entertainment. Such is a precious view, ignorant of the fact that entertainment is as integral to human life as food and sleep. The argument is rather that culture and art, which depend on care, on cultivation over a long period of time, and which exhibit the property that they endure, are being destroyed by being transformed into entertainment goods, subject to the principles of novelty, accessibility and transience; that is, subject to the principles of consumption.

The theatre occupies a special place in a remissive culture. It serves as the art fulcrum for a society that seeks to make social and personal relations more exploratory and autonomously creative than the habit- and custom-governed interactions typical of the old culture. This focus on personal relations awakens a need for social-realist theatre, for a clarifying mirror placed before the now unpredictable, always evolving, modes of human relationship. At the same time social life itself becomes more dramaturgical (and the sociologist, Erving Goffman, who has done most to point this out, has thereby himself gained contemporary celebrity).

Communities bound by morality follow standards of conduct that invest their actions with seriousness and meaningfulness. By contrast a remissive culture finds 'meaning' problematical. It has abolished all meaning apart from hedonistic release; it has cast away all anchors apart from one tying it to a constantly shifting present; it has shunned the moral constraints that give men a sense of where they are and what they should do at those inescapable times when their desires do not speak clearly and strongly. The constant pursuit of immediate pleasure brings the risk of failing to be able to devise novel absorbing games. Dramaturgical behaviour, as children show us, has the advantage that it is normative, in spite of the fact that in not serving any future goal it is encompassed by the present. Drama has the meaning that *form* brings. From children's games to adult theatre it is governed by strict rules inherited from the past, precise traditions of procedure not to be infringed under any circumstances. Drama's content is also meaningful, its action representing more than what simply appears on the surface to be in play. By providing a vehicle for the expression of personal vicissitudes and the easing of social contacts it serves to integrate past, present and future. The closest to seriousness that a hedonist can come is in formalizing his play into theatre, thereby creating for it some sense of transcending the present and belonging to a tradition.

Our transitional culture has other good reasons for incorporating the theatre. Its members will retain strong psychological attachments to old forms. Probably the only way truly to sever such ties is to continue acting out inherited habits and customs, but with progressively greater self-consciousness and more theatrically - thus gaining distance and independence. Remissive-hedonist man seeks to render the action he is disposed to by upbringing more pleasurable: one means is to stage it in the genre of theatre - increase pose, mimicry, gesture, *flâneurie*, repartee, *mise-en-scène*, in for example the manner of the seventeenth- and eighteenth-century

French aristocracy. Moreover, making play of the rituals of the departing culture will also serve the pleasure of nostalgia for the myth-bearing past.

The formal and functional differences are dissolving between the traditional theatre and the street theatre of political demonstration, the psychodrama enacted in 'encounter groups', the mass carnivals of sport, pop music and celebrity intellectuals. Today it is the whole gamut of social life that carries on what opera achieved last century, and film continued earlier this century, to expand the definition of the theatre.

The growing theatricality of modern life is a direct consequence of the erosion of Puritan authority, and in particular of the loss of confidence in vocation. The Puritan past was dynamic: it pioneered, it cultivated, it built. As the commitments of that past fail, so does the will it invested in work, and in play. Inertia grows in the kingdom of work. Individuals withdraw from politics and administration, leaving them to machines and their engineers. Men who labour without purpose become comatose and channel their resentment into gratuitously disruptive behaviour, directed by trade unions, publicised as drama by the media. Histrionics substitute for passion.

Inertia also grows in the kingdom of leisure. Here too the present is vacant, and across its windy spaces men in search of a past that was significant erect model Gold Rush towns and ersatz medieval castles (that is when they do not, in depressive withdrawal, enclose themselves in packaged entertainment). Television too has taken with great success to renovating the past, in dramas simulating Victorian and Edwardian manners, glamorized as firm and coddling. Men who make nothing of archetypal significance to themselves, who live without vocation and therefore without inwardness, gain some release in touring eras in which men were heroes, families were charmed and life was bound. But this is history as entertainment, for it is not called on to illuminate the deeper purposes of a living present; it serves rather the god of forgetfulness, of oblivion, the tranquillizing god. The Western city may be in the process of becoming an automated utilitarian construction of skyscrapers, supermarkets and speedy transit systems servicing a ring of museums, displaying, as both popular and high culture, icons and simulations representative of virtually every human activity from select past epochs. In this utopia men will labour in order to purchase a ticket for a ride in the time machine of passive leisure.

The reign of inertia, over a barren present, is the psychological state of depression. Drudgery is the work of the depressive; leisure is the play of the depressive. The nineteenth-century Decadents, who aspired to live their lives as pose, provide in their moral languor a preview of remissive inertia. These late Romantics, or late Puritans, were already, in the theatricality of their display, remote from binding purposes; but they were not yet inert, in spite of the fact that their literary paradigm, Huysmans' *Des Esseintes*, teetered on the brink of utter passivity. Remissive-hedonism is psychologically one degree cooler than the exquisitely cultivated, aesthetically contrived life-style of the Decadents, who at least had a passion for manner. At the end of the line of Puritan authority, where it lapses completely, is remissive-hedonism, which turns out to be providing symbolic forms for depressive psychological types, an ideology for individuals who are locked into their pasts without an outlook, without the passion to move. This is the ultimate truth about remissive man, that in his maturity he is a depressive, trying to keep afloat by clutching at the straw of hedonist ideology.

5

Paranoia and Cultural Change

Times of cultural upheaval are of themselves conducive to paranoia. The experience of social change that involves the transformation of existing practices and beliefs into radically new ones forces psychic relocation and provokes complex destabilizing anxieties. A social order that has lost authority fails in its function of consolidating the individual's control over his latently anarchic impulses. If that individual is not to succumb to pathology, his own superego, his personal sense of good and evil, must take on extra weight. The resulting psychological milieu will be characterized by strained perceptions of and ties to reality, doubts about the legitimacy of either internalized character or external society, all held together by highly explosive moralism. Discharges of paranoia are inevitable.

Such transitional periods, at least in the case of European history, have tended to generate radical political movements (for instance, millennarian movements), for which, in turn, paranoia proves to be especially functional. Paranoia provides the most efficient means for stimulating and channelling highly charged feelings. It is the ideal vehicle for invigorating illusions about new idols, and indignant hostility towards the old idols - ordering symbols which will necessarily have guarded some virtues and some truths. It is the most reliable of those midwives, cherished by Marx, officiating at the birth of a new culture. No revolutionary group will be equal in militant vitality to the one convinced that it represents the good against persecuting forces of evil that it alone has recognized and specified for what they are. Here is a second factor augmenting the likelihood that periods of decisive cultural transition will favour paranoid perspectives.

There are, additionally, three other factors specific to contemporary Western society, increasing the likelihood of its susceptibility to paranoid outbreaks. First, biological age must be

taken into account in discussing modes of discontent. Youth usually
has a vitality, sustained by buoyant hopes and recurring
excitements, that makes it rarely victim of nihilistic beliefs.
Discontent is more likely to find paranoid channels. On the other
hand, maturity, and certainly that of middle or late age, in
contemporary Western culture, will have an inherent, biological
bias towards nihilism; disenchantment not complemented by
strong hopes or beliefs in alternative communal or individual
purposes, produces feelings of futility rather than persecution,
meaninglessness rather than being trapped, and detachment rather
than alienation. Thus a society in which youth forms the
revolutionary vanguard is likely to experience paranoid political
styles, while one in which the assault on established norms comes
from those older, experiences a climate of change that is in itself
more immediately remissive. The question remains as to why
current cultural change should have been mediated mainly by sons
rather than dissident fathers.

Second, an affluence factor may influence modern political styles
in a paranoid direction. Increasing affluence tends to make its
carriers more vulnerable to threat, less resistant to pain and more
likely to fantasize about violence, in particular the possibility of
violent attacks on themselves. There is truth in the cliché that a man
who has to work hard physically to make his daily bread, and is
absorbed by the task, is unlikely to exhibit neurotic paranoid
symptoms. Within the Puritan tradition paranoia became prevalent
only in the late, more decadent phases of bourgeois utilitarianism.
Here is one tentative line of explanation for the fact that psychiatric
hospitals in the West are today reporting a marked relative increase
in psychosis of a paranoid type.

Third, and most significantly for this analysis, there is a factor
linked directly to the decline of Puritan culture and its
character-type. The Puritan for whom authority fails, who cannot
find his vocation or whose passion is frustrated, must turn against
the forbidding culture whose commands he has failed. What Freud
termed the 'narcissism of minor differences' ensures that the
distance he experiences from the constraints that he has rigorously
internalized will make him turn in resentment against that culture,
which he now reads as persecuting. If the father-exemplar does not
welcome and accept him, the disciple must, like Judas, destroy the
belittling authority. Goethe made the same point in a more general

and affable manner when he said that we are never as hostile to any ideas as those we ourselves have just abandoned. When Puritanism fails in this manner it turns into paranoia: the sense of authority remains equally strong, but the cultural valency is reversed, authority now being perceived as persecuting rather than enabling. Thus a Puritan culture readily turns paranoid, taking its first step in the direction of the remissive. (I do not wish to suggest by concentrating here on paranoia that it is the only psychological state typical of periods of cultural transition. Such periods, in their relaxation of norms, are also conducive to the styles, on the one hand, of charisma and of release, and, on the other, of depression.)

In turning now to specific instances I want to look first at some of the more prominent paranoid critiques of Western society, for their influence has been decisive in the cultural shifts of our time. Paranoia has nowhere manifested itself more clearly as a contemporary catalyst for cultural change than in the popularity of the work of R. D. Laing (more in Britain than the USA where it was figures like Paul Goodman who played an equivalent role). Setting aside the scientific originality and validity of his work, Laing's prominence as the intellectual prophet for a vast following not merely within the confines of academia, and not merely among the ranks of youth, was due to the success with which he clothed one of the central morals of the remissive, the belief in the possibility of complete self-cure and self-change, in fabrics of paranoid aggression. He made it easy for others to banalize his writings into the acutely paranoid view that only the odd, the freakish and the schizophrenic are sane in a society controlled by such evil figures as psychiatrists, such evil instruments as provided by the Western rationalist-scientist tradition, and by such evil structures as the repressive nuclear family. His chiliastic sociology sparked the paranoid indignation necessary to effect the casting off of the quasi-Puritanical morality of the parents, and the instituting of the ideology of the remissive. (The American film *The Graduate* attracted wide popularity in the late 1960s, particularly amongst tertiary students, by a similar paranoid stereotyping of middle-class parents.)

There is a second reason for Laing's great popularity: he was one of the first to feed a growing contemporary interest in schizophrenia. This interest itself requires some explanation. Apart from a new realization that psychosis, often latent or concealed, is widespread in the community, popular concern has been stimulated by two factors. First, the schizophrenic, like his ancestors the Old Testament prophet and the medieval saint, is potentially a far more glamorous figure than the neurotic everyman. Remissive-hedonist man, needing exemplars for narcissistic identification, prefers one he can readily associate with the Romantic tradition of the outsider, the stranger, the misfit, the visionary (thus in part the revival of interest in William Blake).

Second, neurosis, according to Freud, is likely incurable. Its bindings may at best be loosened, and then only by lengthy and painstaking effort. The individual who demands rapid self-change will prefer the psychotic model for at least two reasons: he suspects that the psychotic, especially the visionary type, is in some senses more healthy than anyone else, and he believes, as Laing has taught him, that psychosis is amenable to miracle cure.

Laing, neglecting Freud's work on ambivalence, reintroduced a type of moral dualism. Distorting the Puritan public-private dualism, he developed a Marxist interpretation of social institutions - in particular the contemporary family - as instruments of pure evil. He complemented blanket hostility to public life with a remissive defence of release as the sole means of private virtue.

Laing's 'anti-psychiatry' movement may legitimately claim successes, but their importance has been readily exaggerated. Until recently mental hospitals, like prisons, were institutions that had lagged behind the general twentieth-century trend towards liberalization. Their severe interdictive-punitive nature was out of key with an increasingly remissive society. Consequently, removing the bars had an unnaturally marked impact in terms of the responses of patients. What was illustrated here was not that the first step towards an eventual cure had been achieved, but merely that inmates become more comfortable once certain levels of institutional repression are lowered. The hypothesis is again that to place a Puritan nature in a permissive environment may release imaginative capacities hitherto repressed; but a remitted nature, because of its lack of inner controls, will not justify the same confidence in amelioration.

Laing's work constitutes a half-way house between the paranoid and the remissive, advocating the value-free world of the latter where

nobody is guilty, but nevertheless wanting to blame society.
Herbert Marcuse, tapping the same psychological reflexes,
succeeded for a period of two or three years as the leading prophet of
contemporary society. He provided the young both with an
idealized picture of themselves, gay and polymorphously poetic,
and a paranoid image of a homogeneously repressive society bent on
distorting their capacity to realize the ideal. Marcuse's work does
deal in part in realizable hopes and rational criticisms. But overall it
lacks authority, appearing rather as a rag-bag of ill-co-ordinated
enthusiasms: nostalgia for the old culture, whose prototype he finds
in the aristocratic Weimar of Goethe and Schiller; mystical
yearnings in the vein of Rilke's Orpheus; Marxist disgust at the
money fetish and work alienation combined with hopes for
liberation through automation-served affluence; and Rousseauist
images of the noble instinctual savage. The other modern American
evangelist of cultural psychology, Norman Brown, has been less
confused in his affiliations. Showing little sympathy for the
authority of the old culture, immune to the call of paranoid
Marxism, he is the true prophet of the remissive, proclaiming the
creed to end all creeds, that of panacean eros.

   In spite of some recognition of Freud's equation of culture with
instinctual renunciation, the tone of Marcuse's work remains naively
Rousseauist. There is no ambivalence in the attack on existing
Western society; there is no reservation in the advocacy of
community founded on principles of play and display, beauty and
joy - rather Marcuse finds here the final and perfect synthesis of all
the contradictory forces, in both the domains of theory and practice,
that have constituted Western history. His *Eros and Civilization* is a
milestone in the rise of remissive-hedonist ideology, endowing it
with a spurious (in the sense of paranoid) historical genealogy. The
generation of fathers may have unwittingly polluted as they
exploited, but to cast them unambivalently as devils, as to interpret
the immediate past as abysmally black, is irrational. Marcuse
expresses a generalized hostility to the present, rationalized through
lengthy argument. Paranoia, as a delusional type of pathology,
often manifests itself in highly intellectualized forms.

Symptomatic of the same pattern of cultural change is the
prominence of interest in deviancy in the most sought-after of
today's academic disciplines, sociology. The sociology of deviance

articulates paranoid impulses to the degree, and it is marked, that its denizens idealize the abnormal and over-emphasize their ill-treatment at the hands of society's central institutions. Here is another legitimated outlet for Romantic adolescent identification with the misfit, in this case the criminal, the delinquent, the insane, the racially discriminated, the poor, the handicapped, the alienated.

On the other hand, where the sociologist of deviance is governed by voyeurist motives, playing the role of zoo-keeper, as one modern observer has put it, he is representative of the remissive. His activity fulfils at least two remissive functions: it satisfies one of his own leading desires, and it provides technical knowledge necessary for the implementation of facilities for the greater *wel-fare* of the deviant.

Many observations might, obviously, be made about the powerful protest movement that grew up in opposition to American involvement in the Vietnam War. From the strategic argument that this war was militarily impossible for the USA to win, to the pragmatic humanitarian argument that if the USA did win then that victory would be of too little significance to justify its cost in terms of human misery, there were rational dimensions to the Western protest. There were also prominent paranoid dimensions, and it is to these that I wish to draw attention.

The one supreme political authority existing in the Western world today is the American state, industrial and governmental. As such it stands as the leading target for left-oriented protest paranoia (as it does for that paranoia outside its territory expressed as 'anti-Americanism'). The anti-American forces in Vietnam, the 'liberation army', the patron state of North Vietnam and its visible leader Ho Chi Minh were cast as messiahs, crusaders who had to be supported in their holy war, because they were in effect fighting the same war against the same enemy as the raging Western filials. The youth that dominated this movement, having grown up feeling psychologically pariah, aspired to public, social pariahdom, at least ideologically. It applied remissive Christian values to politics, thus flouting Machiavelli's principal thesis that personal and civic moralities are often necessarily incompatible. World politics became the arena for personal remission, through the psychological mechanism of projection (paranoid projection is not new to the

history of politics, where Napoleonic megalomania has provided
merely the most obvious example). What was singular about the
recent case was the division within the nation by which a large and
influential stratum defined itself politically by identifying with the
nation's potential enemies.

The current of remissive feeling now runs so deeply in the USA
that one of the major media networks, CBS, in its documentary
account of the war telecast in the first days after the fall of Saigon,
made no attempt to report the political considerations that had led
to American involvement, but concentrated on private human
plight, on the one hand that of the civilian population, the wasting
of their homes and villages, the maiming and killing of their kin,
and on the other that of the American soldiers, in particular their
sense of futility and fear. The media fuses with its public and
transmits paranoid hostility against the tyrant, in the form of
unrelieved sympathy for its powerless victims. Remissive and
paranoid meet: the lack of realism of the remissive critique of
Realpolitik adds volume to the free-surging moral indignation of
the paranoid, projecting his own hostile impulses, unperturbed
whether or not the projected scenario fits the events on which it is
posed.

The pre-eminent manifestation in the last decade of a culture in flux
was the student movement, which first appeared at Berkeley in
1964. By 1968, the zenith, it had built up a momentum of
consequence throughout the Western world. The pathology at the
root of this movement has been most thoroughly explored by Lewis
Feuer, who, in his historical study, *The Conflict of Generations*,
argues that the psychological theme of generational revolt has been
common to all student agitations, whether Russian, German,
French, Japanese or American, whether this century or last, whether
of the left or the right. Feuer's thesis is that sons in revolt against
fathers project their oedipal resentment into the public spheres of
the university and the society at large.

The following quotation from a student article published in
November 1965, at Berkeley, sums up the case that Feuer puts at
length:

> In many ways this student generation is healthy and is free from
> many of the racial, sexual, class and cultural straitjackets of
> middle-class America. . . .

Yet intermingled with these healthy trends is a strong strain of sheer Nihilism. The Campus Left is crawling with Nihilists - who discharge their personal hostilities and frustrations beneath the mask of radical politics.

Haven't you seen the people who talk of 'peace' and 'non-violence' with hatred glowing in their eyes? Haven't you noticed that many who shout of 'human brotherhood' are cool and calculating in their personal relations?

Haven't you seen the people who wear 'free speech' buttons while they heckle, jeer and laugh at speakers with whom they disagree? Haven't you noticed the people who talk of 'civil rights' but hound any Negro as an 'Uncle Tom' if he doesn't agree with their militant politics?

And haven't you seen people who scream insults and epithets at police, accusing the police of 'police brutality' while they deliberately attempt to provoke the police into committing brutality? You haven't seen them? Where have you been in the past few years? . . . But the Nihilists are destructive for the sake of destruction . . . they are anti-American, anti-government, anti-liberal, anti-moderate, anti-Peace Corps, anti-University.

They attack the 'Establishment', whether L.B.J. or the University - simply because it is an establishment, simply because it is authority. American institutions are attacked as tyrannical and University rules on speech as 'atrocities' but the Nihilists never mention the slaughter of Hungarians by the Soviet Union or the 'thought control' in Communist China.

Here is paranoid irrationality, in the most familiar of that pathology's guises: parricide. Revolt is the leading motive; genuine sympathy for blacks, or the poor, or genuine interest in making the university a better educational institution, are present at the most as weak and fleeting enthusiasms. The style of action that is sought is the euphoric drama of the crowd rather than the hard grind of practical politics. The call for 'participatory democracy' hides an élitist totalitarianism, a new order to be run by all-powerful students, tolerant only of those of like passions. The movement exhibits, on the one hand, delusions of persecution, of all the weak and isolated by all the strong and organized. On the other hand it exhibits delusions of grandeur, vastly exaggerated expectations about its own power of influence.

Qualifications need making to Feuer's argument. They fall into two camps. First, other factors influenced the specific situations in which student unrest surfaced. In some cases students had good reason for complaint. The Sorbonne, for example, was not the only university whose size, remoteness and casualness made serious study and a decent student life virtually impossible. There were cases in which university authorities over-reacted to minor student grievances, and in which the police were vigorous if not brutal.

Second, historical factors must be taken into account in discussing why student unrest broke out in precisely this period, and why it took on a paranoid form. In particular, attention needs to be focused on the anxieties aroused in the offspring of affluent middle-class backgrounds by the transition from Puritan to remissive cultures. Such is my interest at this point.

The question arises from the outset of whether generational conflict is catalysed by the presence of weak or tyrannical fathers. Feuer produces evidence suggesting that the nineteenth-century Russian movement was emotionally funded by hostility to weak fathers, effete liberals as portrayed in Turgenev's *Fathers and Sons* (and Dostoevsky's *The Possessed*): sons are shown in revolt against becoming like their fathers. Erikson puts a similar case in his *Childhood and Society*, arguing that German youth in the 1920s and 1930s responded to Hitler's cry that they had been betrayed by weak fathers, senile old men, who had capitulated both to the tedium of modern decadent society and to the enemy of 1914-18. But the German case is more complex, if, as Erikson argues, the fathers were themselves domineering, fitting the 'authoritarian personality' syndrome of acting tyrannically when in positions of authority, submissively when not.

The American pattern appears more like the Russian than the German. Margaret Mead, in her *Male and Female* (1949), and Erik Erikson, in his *Childhood and Society* (1950), both typed the American family as having a weak father. Mead writes of the absence of a father whose awareness of his own masculinity makes him feel his small masculine son as a threat and a challenge; the American father is, by contrast, admiring, helpful, over-protective, identifying with his son. Erikson claims that in working as a psychoanalyst with American men it takes considerable time to break through to the insight that there was a period early in life when the father did seem bigger and threatening. Mead and

Erikson's portrait of the American family is that caricatured in popular literature: the meek, hen-pecked husband enslaved by the strident, powerful wife. It is Dos Passos's picture of Mac and Maisie in *U.S.A.*; it is Philip Roth's picture of the narrator's family in *Letting Go*.

Kenneth Keniston, in *The Uncommitted* (1965), *Young Radicals* (1968), and *Youth and Dissent* (1971) provides an analysis of youth and the student movement that draws on a range of empirical studies carried out during the 1960s. His general psychological conclusions confirm the more speculatively based picture of the American family that Mead and Erikson had sketched. In Keniston's own studies of both 'alienated' (uncommitted, depressive) and politically radical students, the patterns of family background are remarkably similar: the mother dominant, possessive, over-soliciting, emotional; the father detached and ineffectual. In the case of greater importance to us here - that of the radicals - there was one difference, the suggestion of filial ambivalence towards the father. While the father was despised as weak, he was alternatively often respected for being a man of principle. The parents of radicals were usually intellectually liberal, disenchanted with business and its values, and warm and supportive in relation to their son, but not in relation to each other; and they stressed success. The sons emerged highly committed to principles, with a sense of their own special qualities, and of the superiority of themselves and their families over the surrounding community.

There are psychological connections that ought to be noted at this point. Freudian theory holds that the oedipal situation distorted by a dominating mother and a weak father has a tendency to produce homosexual sons. Freud writes also of a link he found repeatedly in his clinical work between paranoia and homosexuality. There are thus psychoanalytical grounds for expecting paranoid rebellion to emerge amongst sons who experience their fathers as failures. Keniston's radicals had in the main lived their adolescence under strain, withdrawn and intellectual; a minority had developed extreme neurotic symptoms, including paranoia, in late adolescence.

I do not wish to stress the psychoanalytic conjecture. I am more concerned to pursue the theme of failed authority. To the degree that the picture of the American family as effectively fatherless is valid, there will be an overwhelming problem of legitimacy for sons.

A vacuum of authority is created in the fraught time between childhood/adolescence and adulthood, when example and guidance are desperately sought, when the need for identification is peculiarly intense. Resentment is inevitable, towards family and society that have failed to impose credible commands.

The resentment will be acute for the sons of the affluent middle class, no longer absorbed by the purposes of upward social mobility. Materially secure, raised on Romantic myths encouraging them to fantasize about their own heroic omnipotence, they have the leisure of college years in which to tangle irresponsibly with their passions. Keniston's radicals often felt that they were wasting life, that they were at the end of the line; they found in politics a sense of collective purpose. They were singular amongst other students for their unusually strong commitments and their unusually few specific plans. Durkheim categorized this state as *egoism*: whatever the individual's principles, his passions lack the control and direction provided only by effective social bonds, and hence degenerate into a chaos of unsettled impulses. Without exemplars, these students could not find vocation, the means by which principled passion might fuse with social purpose. While their ideology was one of superiority, commitment and success, they felt psychologically pariah, abandoned, uncalled, condemned to the role of a Theseus without an Ariadne, a Telemachus without an Odysseus, an Achilles without a Trojan War, above all a Paul without the example of a Christ.

The parental stress on success might be linked with the Puritan's stress on excellence. But the former is an abstract command: it would become meaningful for the son only if he saw his parents, and in particular his father, living by the same command, and exemplary in obedience to it. Likewise, the son might see himself in the role of the hero, who traditionally is fatherless, or at least of obscure origins. But again the identification is abstract, for real messiahs require the rigours of discipleship before they are ready to don the robes of genuine authority.

My thesis here draws on the old maxim, argued by Machiavelli, illustrated by medieval history, that peoples do not rise up against strong tyrants, but against weak kings. Tocqueville insisted that the French Revolution did not bring down the *Ancien Régime*, but the decline of the *Ancien Régime* brought on the French Revolution. Feuer points out that Berkeley, the setting for the formative modern revolt, was staffed by probably the most liberal faculty in the USA. Student ideology focused on the 'liberal' as one of its favourite targets; its attack was precisely in terms of the liberal's effeteness, his lack of authority. And as if playing right into the dissenters' hands, the Berkeley faculty voted in favour of their demands, capitulating, and in some cases overtly admiring the stampeding youth.

This may, at one level, be generational revolt, but it is revolt in search of exemplars, and if the heroes of liberal democracy do not bear respect then, *faute de mieux*, more extreme fathers will be sought. The turn is not from realistic to charismatic politics, a facile distinction, but one away from a politics whose charisma has failed. And the students chose as one of their ideals the most authoritative of all modern political fathers. Mao Tse-tung has been portrayed in the West as the great patriarch who led his people through danger to safety and prosperity. He was seen as wise, both in a philosphical and practical manner, benign, ineffable, distant, and all-powerful - the modern Moses. Moses, significantly, was the historical figure that Freud himself took as the paradigm of authority.

The governing psychological dynamic is internalization of parental nihilism. For the parent's generation a lurking aimlessness was camouflaged by economic necessity, which successfully kept buoyant the pervasive ideology of building a liberal-democratic society founded on consumer affluence. But the ideology was forced, false beneath its power to tranquillize the terror of incipient nihilism. It confirmed the parent in a dissatisfying life in which he (or she) split himself into a bad character, himself, who atoned through self-sacrifice in work and belief for the benefit of the good character, the child, his one worthy creation. The good child had to be cossetted from the savage realities of public life, fed on Romantic myths about the evil of a world that would work to corrupt his own unique virtue. The child had to be protected from the tentacled finitude of the world that had crushed the parent's aspirations, made the parent suffer guilt for his own failure, which he now attempted to redeem by inverting it into an identification with the future success of his child. The child was brought up rewarded consistently for one thing, his successes, principally at school. The values of character, kindness and civic conscience were deflated in favour of a megalomanic vision (no wonder that the child in late adolescence would be prone to paranoia). That child's fantasies about his own omnipotence were indulged, cultivated; he was told that even he could be President, with the thinly cushioned jab that anything less and he would not be worthy, he would have let the parent down and failed, in his turn, to atone for all the sacrifice. A film about the Harvard Law School, *The Paper Chase*, caught well the pressures of the upbringing, and the murderous consequences of failure. And the successes remained of uneasy satisfaction, for they took the form of the child pleasing the parent, not of the child finding his vocation and thereby his adulthood, finding his own sense of independent presence, and authority.

As significant in this psychological web as the failure of the father was the different failure of the mother and the role she came to play as the perpetrator of guilt. The father, depressed by his inability to live in terms of the vague ideals that had borne him lightly through adolescence, favoured escape through regression into fraternal camaraderie, in his clubs, at his work, with his sons. The mother, on the other hand, restless in a home that failed to absorb her passions, manipulated both father and son in her anxiety. She ensnared the former in the guilt of inadequacy, the latter in the guilt of sacrifice - that he, the son, was the cause for her costly self-sacrifice, and woe betide him should he fail, either in his vocation or in his devotion, and woe betide him in any case. The father's nihilism spelt melancholic withdrawal, the mother's hysterical manipulation.

The woman's failure to find ease in any of her roles - wife, mother or professional - necessarily affected her child. The inheritance she passed on was heavily coloured by loss of Puritan confidence in her own judgment; a loss illustrated at one level by her need for manuals instructing her how to meet every crisis, major or minor, involved in bringing up a child; illustrated at another level by her asking the public world for standards by which to measure that child's worthiness. The consequences were definitive. For instance, by demanding that her son be Galahad pure, yet failing to transmit faith in the social order that the knight should champion, she ensured that when the guilty son rose against that order, as he would, he would do so by paranoid defiling, cursing it in the language of excrement, littering its halls, as happened notably during the occupation of Columbia University, with the refuse of remiss living.

Contemporary students, Bruno Bettelheim argues in his article 'Obsolete Youth', fear that technology, in displacing the possibility of meaningful work, has made them redundant. They suffer, in addition, from postponed maturity, forced to spend many years in college and university when they would rather be involved in responsible and challenging work. Prima facie this case does not hold, for it was precisely the sons of the affluent middle class, with seemingly unprecedentedly secure futures in terms of ready access to power and wealth, who occupied the centre of radical politics. And the period was one of high economic prosperity, with little threat of careers becoming scarce. Worsening economic conditions in the early 1970s coincided with the waning of student unrest, events partly connected, as fears for the future dampened cavalier discontent. Moreover, the fathers of these sons themselves went to college, hence prolonging their adolescences; yet they did not revolt, or certainly not to the same degree. The solid majority of the student body, whose fathers were without tertiary education, were not those who drove the modern movement.

Student dissent, to continue the theme of prolonged adolescence, did exhibit itself in part as the revolt of the dependent in support of other dependents - the poor, the weak, the discriminated. The generation of fathers did not revolt in the corresponding situation of dependency because they saw their education as instrumental to a commanding goal. Dependency in universities is a problem only when it does not point beyond itself.

The case for obsolete youth carries the inference that the nature of work has changed. But shifts in the range of available tasks have not been sudden or pervasive enough alone to have precipitated anomic hostility of the intensity of the last decade. More important to recognize here is that the psychological factor of vocation having lost its legitimacy combined with the sociological factor of economic necessity failing to operate as a surrogate incentive. The jobs that keep modern industrial societies functioning have lost their attraction, and inevitably so, given that the framing culture, and its priests, have lost their authority. It is not that the goals of suburbia and a successful business career are in themselves paltry, but that the culture has failed to support them. Two conditions must be satisfied for work to have value. Work must be fulfilling for the individual, a condition which depends in turn on that individual's disposition; and second, work itself must have charisma, it must command social virtue. This latter charisma is a mode of authority established in indispensable part through inheritance from a master, whose presence and competence make the work holy in the eyes of the apprentice. The master/apprentice model applies not only to crafts, but to all forms of vocation, from the professions and business to the various trades.

The genre of interpretation that I am employing is constantly in danger of finding its universals tangled up with its particulars, their multiple distances and weights out of hand. To give but one example, which ought to be addressed at this point: it may be universal to Western society and its history, certainly to its recent history, that adolescence, especially for males, is a biographical phase normally fraught with traits of behaviour and belief that are typically paranoid. What does it mean then to discuss the student movement of the 1960s as an historical particular? Certainly, universal elements of strained adolescence were decisive to this movement, but because of the specific nature of the situation they became amplified, and joined with other forces, to produce consequences of far greater significance than could normally have been expected. These consequences were not restricted to temporary tensions within individual families, or students having one or two unexpectedly poor years at university. They contributed to a larger historical momentum, in which the general forms of institutions and conduct were at issue. And although, for many of the students, these years proved to be transitional, as in normal adolescence, transforming eventually into the maturity that is founded on realistic perceptions, the movement in which they participated exerted more than passing influence. Its paranoia served as a catalyst for innovating the remissive style, or more accurately, for consolidating and democratizing, in the sense of deconverting quasi-Puritans in far greater numbers, the movement that has been carried by individuals and small groups since Nietzsche. The bohemians of the 1950s can no longer claim to be 'outsiders'; with their literary hero, Meursault, they have become commonplace, the normative majority on most campuses, the emerging suburban exemplars, partly adapted, of an antidote to bourgeois ennui.

My intention in this extended discussion of the student movement of the 1960s has not been to qualify the decisive role that paranoia played. It has been rather to clarify the psychological and sociological dimensions of paranoid revolt, and in particular to spell out its links with the decline of Puritan authority. The discussion should also have served to make the point, which could equally well be made in each of the examples of paranoid behaviour used in this essay, that any social phenomenon or event has many components and many determinants. I have argued for paranoia as a dominant element, common to the different examples.

The discussion of student movements raises a general question about politics. Feuer wants to argue that irrational politics, in particular that motivated by generational revolt, cannot produce good. He cites the reactionary backlash provoked in Russia by the student assassination of Alexander II, who had been in the process of establishing proceedings for the writing of a constitution. He argues that the consequences of Berkeley were threefold: an increase in violence and lawlessness throughout the USA, an increasing anti-intellectualism, especially in California, and a lowering of the level of the country's political ethics. This weight of generalization will not stand up. For instance, the same movement may have been responsible for the gain of shortening the Vietnam war. Whatever the details, Machiavelli's maxim holds, that in politics evil may beget good, and good evil; and the long-term consequences of recent events cannot be gauged. Moreover, the kinds of irrational element that Feuer isolates are present in all politics, although he might plausibly argue, usually to a less contaminating degree.

The preference I have shown for Puritan politics is not based on the belief that they are perfectly rational. On the contrary, the Puritan for whom politics is a vocation was driven by the pursuit of salvation, an other-worldly, religious, 'irrational' end. His rationality was conditioned by his theology and by his disposition. His insistence in the public world on explicitness, honesty, self-control, scrupulous calculation, virtues that we have come to identify with 'liberal, rational politics', was in itself a rationalization of his own need for control, of his own theory of vocation. That this public style was successful, in economic and political terms, suggests that it did enable a more realistic grasp of the material world than had alternative cultural orientations. It was viable in both individual and communal terms. My preference then operates at two levels. The first is rational: some Puritan traits are necessary for our survival, both in maintaining the economic vitality on which social and military security depends, and in maintaining a sense of purpose and belonging for men who are still Puritan by disposition and who have not the resources to establish an alternative culture that is viable. The maintenance of economic vitality requires methods that are 'rational' in another sense, that of the efficient realization of predetermined ends, ends themselves that have been decided on the basis of realistic perceptions of the world at large. The second level of preference is aesthetic. Ultimately our preferences are governed by our own dispositions and their chosen cultural forms: certain styles of behaviour simply look more attractive to us than others. Viewed from either level, paranoid politics appears threateningly uncontrolled.

In the wake of outbursts of an unprecedented militancy against the bourgeois/Puritan ethos there are signs of a shift from paranoid to remissive. The utopian and Marxist ideal is at last coming to fruition. The bourgeois fathers have lost their power to command. Moreover the state, in terms of its most publicly felt traditional power, its capacity to limit the range of any individual's pleasures, is in the process of withering away. As egalitarian ideals are more fully realized, and the bourgeois life-style becomes accessible to the many, that style itself transforms into its final stage, that of the remissive. Correspondingly, that bourgeois phenomenon, the anti-bourgeois rebel, has been democratized. Now everyman can be a *Steppenwolf* - Hesse's Romantic tale for the middle-brow echelons of the cultural élite of 1927 was rediscovered by the hippie every-youth of the late 1960s.

The extraordinary popularity in 1973-4 of Blatty's book *The Exorcist*, and its film version, may have been due to the success with which it played upon middle-class paranoia. The work portrays a normal home, cushioned in all the comforts of high bourgeois affluence, suddenly and gratuitously struck with a case of demonic possession (that the mother, not a-typical of her class, under pressure is an hysteric, is the single factor which might tenuously be forwarded as a cause for the daughter's 'disease'). Science, the magic wand maintaining bourgeois security, here taking the form of modern medicine and psychiatry, shown at its best, proves impotent. The last resort is a regression to the Church and one of its ancient occult rituals. *The Exorcist* exploits the fear that the order presiding in the affluent suburbs of contemporary society is brittle, that however tightly stable it seems on the surface, it is inwardly vulnerable to some vast irrational force from beyond shattering it. While this fear and its projected doom fantasies are probably common to all civilized communities, in their specific form here they reflect an insecurity at the psychic core of bourgeois society, a cardinal symptom of that order in decline, its Puritan confidence petrified, its vitality transformed into an hysterical attempt to batten the windows of a house which turns out to be built on quicksand. Again it is paranoia that seeps in to fill the shell of failing inner authority.

Another phenomenon generating extraordinary appeal in the early 1970s has been the Divine Light Mission. It has proved to be the most enduring and popular of recent religious cults. Its converts have been the youth that in many cases had become disaffected with radical politics and the less ascetic modes of the 'counter-culture'. Its hallmark has been paranoid images of an evil society on the edge of a millennium, cast in a language which has far more in common with the cruder genres of American advertising than Eastern mysticism. It is not simply the size of the movement that is remarkable, but its success in attracting the highly educated and professionally successful for whom all other gods, and notably the more subtle and demanding ones, had failed. Divine Light provides paranoid community, a home secure from loneliness, failure and futility, a crèche unified and protected by delusions of grandeur about itself and its guru, and by delusions about the evil outside.

The Puritan preacher castigated his own congregation. It was the members themselves of that congregation who were vulnerable; their moral power and responsibility was over and to themselves. The Guru Maharaj Ji, presiding over Divine Light, typifies the post-Puritan paranoid era in his praise of his brethren and condemnation of the unenlightened. Whoever seeks remissive-hedonist culture will find priests who praise him merely for his interest, who console him for his origins, who are not concerned at the inconsistency of his works or the slowness of his progress; he will find music also which soothes rather than exhorts. The first law of remissive-hedonist doctrine is that self-criticism is neurotic.

The radical politics of the student movement and the passive withdrawal of the Divine Light Mission represent the poles of youth paranoia during the decade. While the imagery of both was paranoid, their behaviour varied. The Mission was typical of the many groups that sought to escape from the society's central institutions rather than confront them, groups that hoped to establish anarcho-syndicalist community, groups that chose private, often drug-induced withdrawal. Paranoid perceptions fused with remissive conduct. And whereas the radical student was paranoid in act, the convert to anti-political sects was more likely to be depressive.

No new political thrust has been as tenaciously active in the West since the early 1970s as that dedicated to preserving the natural environment. While the movement for ecological conservation has been in part rational, having as one of its ultimate goals the preservation of the species, it has nevertheless exhibited classical paranoid traits. It feeds off the persecution phobia of death by poisoning. The scenario is of ubiquitous forces infesting the wood of society's house, conspiring to contaminate the air, lakes, rivers, seas and fertile land with evil effluent, to poison food with chemicals, removing the *good*, natural, life-nourishing elements. In Shakespeare's day the Thames stank; at the Versailles of *le roi soleil* the corridors reeked of human urine, the palace walls were caked with human excrement, emptied by the bucket from the windows; diet has progressively improved for rich and poor alike, since the middle ages when the former gorged routinely on undressed meat, and the latter lived on gruel.

Marxist demonology teems. The corporation, the manager, the capitalist system are the forces of evil, illicitly poisoning the good people, whose last hope is to be rescued by a State devoted to servicing welfare. Here is another manifestation of public paranoia, another flank on which to attack inherited authority, part of a general *lèse-majesté* in the face of failing constraints, part of a widespread movement from Puritan to remissive. For the Puritan, nature was a wilderness, to be fashioned at will by man's godly hand. Now that the authority guiding that hand is in disrepute, the sins of the fathers must be expiated.

The movement is reminiscent, on the other hand, of upper-middle-class attempts earlier this century to find new privileges to replace those eclipsed by the increasing affluence that produced the mass market, and made, for instance, cars, telephones and reasonable quality clothing available to the many. Fastidious taste is an orthodox bourgeois strategy for establishing social uniqueness; refinement and expertise about nutritional ingredients is merely one of its contemporary manifestations. However, there is a crucial difference: the explicit ideology of the environmentalists does not stress new levels of status, whatever the more Puritan undertones about discriminating knowledge. On the contrary, it is remissive: the ideology asserts that all men are victims. The battle lines are not drawn according to social class, at least on the plane of ideology, but between an abstract social system and its dependants, rich and poor alike. The shift in power, as generally through the economy, is from the machines of industry and their entrepreneurs to knowledge, the former creating the ills to be cured by the latter.

While the environmentalist creed is egalitarian, it is preached almost exclusively by the highly educated citizens of affluent suburbs. The class bias in the movement is further illustrated by the prominence of the purity archetype, in a new garb. Perhaps the fastidious bourgeois, in finding his work less absorbing, in needing substitute outlets for his notorious anal compulsiveness, turns his control addiction on to his physical environment, demanding that it be systematically cleansed.

The individual who suffers from chronic paranoia has periods when he cannot move; every new situation is infested with potential threats; he finds it safer to remain inert, totally removed, as he is by his insistent fantasies, from reality. So it is also for a society. The environmentalist movement compounds dangerously irrational traits emerging in contemporary Western society: it is another symptom of a political climate in which it becomes progressively more difficult for any economic institution to move without provoking widespread fears that it will wreak evil. Industry is blamed first, analysed after. Pipelines may not be laid, supersonic jets may not be flown, power stations may not be built, just in case. Great resources of energy and intelligence are being turned against productive enterprises; it is politically suicidal for a society, for a civilization, to have many of its most capable sons devoted in effect to eroding its economic vitality. A society at war with itself like this is bound for inertia, its creative drives squandered in internal frictions. This time the imagery of social entropy has a threatening plausibility.

I have concentrated on paranoia in its poisoning mode. However, the environmentalist movement is also infected by paranoia of the more general kind, the paranoia of radical politics, which curses whatever exists, and curses especially the established order of commands and constraints; in particular it was that same anarchist paranoia that enthused a range of disaffected politics through the decade, from Vietnam protest to the student disciples of Laing and Marcuse and the metapolitics of the 'counter-culture'. This decade appears as peculiarly paranoid when one considers the accumulated diversity, intensity and persistence of the revolt against inherited authority. It provides a range of chastening illustrations of the hostility to political forms, on the grounds that they impede easy and present gratifications, that Tocqueville predicted would be an inevitable outgrowth of democracy.

I have been mainly concerned with paranoid behaviour that has had its sources in the universities - environmentalism, Vietnam War protest, hostility to current psychiatry, the student movement. It was not simply that left-oriented, university-based extremism has been peculiarly salient in the last decade. My interest has been as much to illustrate the degree to which magic displaced reason as the principal currency sought in our seats of highest learning. This magic came in the form of conspiracy theories, tales about wicked authority and promises of a politics of ecstasy that would level all discriminations and open the gates to the golden age of the natural man. It worked by stoking moral indignation and igniting absurd hopes. Paranoia in the universities, given the influence they have today, constituted a far more serious social problem than paranoia anywhere else, for it was the universities that should have been preparing the few who would carry on the painstaking work of reason, the patient building and renovating of those institutions and customs that compose the backbone of civilization. Instead they became the breweries of remissive ideology, distributing throughout society seductive promises of an easy rise. Their brew lacked a crucial ingredient, what David Hume in his critique of that proto-remissive, John Locke, was at pains to explicate as 'human nature'. One of reason's principal tasks is to come to terms with 'human nature', and there included the prevailing character disposition of the time. Only when that task is near completion does it make sense to start thinking through what changes to the social order might be for the best.

One catalyst for paranoia is the discomfort provoked in an individual by trying to realize an ideal that does not fit him. The paranoid denies that he has limitations of personal capacity imposed by character. Consequently, when he has difficulty achieving his ideals he projects his frustration in aggression against the external agents he views as holding him back. Paranoia of this genus is common today, one of its predominant psychological origins being the situation of a Puritan disposition vainly seeking salvation in a remissive ethic. Many of the participants of radical contemporary social movements, from those pursuing female emancipation to those claiming to be apolitical, carry with their remissive aspirations the damning marks of their Puritan forebears. Their nature condemns them to a Romantic yearning for the 'one true love' and the 'life work', ascetic passions that incapacitate them in relation to their remissive striving to live an untrammelled hedonism. They are victims of an historical cultural transition, and many will never enjoy more than the pleasure of the paranoid outburst, carrying with it too much guilt to be other than an inherently frustrating type of release.

Paranoia would not have reached its degree of prominence in contemporary life without the contribution that the mass media has made to distancing reality. We need to take even more seriously today the devastating critique of the Viennese satirist Karl Kraus. Kraus argued that a society in which language is used carelessly will be careless in all its operations; slovenliness of speech is symptomatic of a corrupt society, casually inhuman in its everyday life. At the root of all evil is the enormously powerful press, inevitably corrupt, with no commitment to reporting the truth, devoted rather to magnifying prejudice, distorting and even inventing 'facts' to suit its own interests. In short, argued Kraus, the press cultivates hysteria and extremism, ensuring that politics will be irrational. Kraus attacked the German Romantic poet Heine for reducing culture to journalism: '[he] has so loosened the corsets of the German language that today every little merchant can fondle her breasts.'

Mediation implies distance. The phenomenal strengthening of the power of the mass media this century has proved a key variable in the increasing remoteness at which a citizen lives from the social and political events that fashion his environment. A fraction only of that media is committed to bridging this distance with the dispassionate, informed reporting and analysis that is prerequisite to a rational and humane social life. Indeed the media's stock-in-trade is exaggeration, the blowing-up of events selected according to the principle of whether they play upon the more extreme fantasies of a

major section of the spectators. Hunter S. Thompson has shown
how much the nation-wide scare in America about the Hell's Angels
motorcycle gang and their orgies of pillaging, violence and rape was
the fictitious creation of the mass media. The media trades in
private fears, it creates facts to fund everyman's paranoid fantasies,
giving them the semblance of reality. By its sensationalist selection
and reporting of news, by its immoderate ethos of constant
high-pitched moral indignation, it creates disasters, catalyses
violence and fosters gossip and tantrum politics. Again Kraus: '[The
press] not only makes the claim that its reports of events are the real
events, it actually achieves this uncanny identity which constantly
creates the impression that deeds must first be reported before they
can be committed. When it publishes lies about atrocities, they
become atrocities.'

Responsible mediation independent from the organs of direct
political power was less necessary when a substantial distance
separated those who governed from those who were governed, when
concomitantly high and low cultures were of different species. Then
there was a good chance that politics would be independent from
the fickle enthusiasms of popular opinion. But with social distance
reduced, and substituted by the distorting distance that the media
force, the presence of a serious and influential press is crucial. Kraus
was right to single out the so-called 'serious' press for attack. Every
modern society needs its popular culture and entertainment and
therefore its popular media, which is relatively honest in its aims; it
equally needs high culture, and a serious media with its own
standards, serving its own functions.

The decline of Puritan authority has had as one of its dimensions
public intrusion on privacy, especially on that of men of affairs. The
USA has gone so far that the Senate and the media now consider it
their national duty to inspect the private financial and personal life
of a candidate (Nelson Rockefeller) for the post of Vice-President.
More would have been learnt of relevancy to his suitability for the
position from his public record in politics. Candidates for major
public office in the USA today cannot afford to have a private life if
they want to become popular enough to be elected; to be public
they must be wholly visible. The demand made of them is that they
conform to the pattern established by those other leading celebrity
figures, the film stars, that they thus conform to the dictates of
popular culture. The public demands to know everything. This is

not simple curiosity: that public wants in particular to be able to gossip about the ordinariness of the extraordinary, it needs to undermine any suggestion of exemplary living. Tocqueville noted that democracies necessarily foster resentments, for they stimulate aspirations to equality that they can never satisfy. Such resentment focuses today, in part as envy, in part as rank hostility, against anyone who moves to occupy a place of authority, anyone whose bearing suggests that they are privileged. The demand to know every private detail of a public figure's past issues from resentment, a paranoid symptom of hostility to authority, which it seeks to discredit. Film stars are usually only too happy to act out the part asked of them; they prefer to live in as contrived and exhibitionistic a manner privately as publicly, needing the type of legitimacy bestowed by visibility to seemingly reverent interest. But actors are not necessarily the more professionally competent for being men of character. The case is quite different for national leaders.

Paranoid fantasies stimulate a range of defensive strategies. In the cases discussed so far, fantasy and the behaviour it manages have exhibited a relatively clear congruency with the paranoid model. There are other spheres of social life, however, in which behaviour, while not explicitly revealing a psychological dynamic of exaggerated fears of persecution, is irrational in a manner suggesting that paranoid mechanisms might be at work. I wish to discuss two connected spheres of this type.

First, the dominant mode of thinking, about nature and about man, which has come to be summed up as 'positivism', belongs here. A more general psychological statement needs to be made at the outset: positivism, in particular in the human sciences, is an intellectual defence against the fear of chaos, of loss of control, of madness. Its reduction of all explanation to the true-false duality, its wielding of Occam's razor to cut itself off from the tantalizing elusiveness of precise non-trivial understandings, in short its casting out of the mind of troubling questions is the product of an obsessive drive for control. But it is possible to be more specific: the threat of nihilism reduces, at least in part, to the paranoid dread that hostile forces will break through from the outside and demolish the individual's sense of himself as a purposive being managing in a predictable world. Hence the need for an ideological cage in which to hide from those forces that cannot be explained, and therefore

rendered manageable, in precise and reliable terms. The governing
rationalization is that if such forces are not consciously recognized
they do not exist: out of sight, out of threat. However,
rationalizations are never deeply convincing. The fear remains,
although plated over, and acts to intensify the zeal with which the
armour of dogma is forged. This strategy works in part because
indeed these forces do not exist as real external threats; they do,
however, exist internally. The extreme positivist is vulnerable then
both to internal destructive impulses, whose expression is restricted
to their displacement into ideology, and to the general situation he
creates for himself, of living in a world over which he has very little
realistic control. This situation courts the danger of becoming a
vicious circle, with a paranoid accelerator at the centre. Unlike other
cases of paranoia, fears do not emerge in explicit form; but the
psychological pattern is the same, with the positivist acting in panic,
as if he were in extreme danger from without. His reaction is purely
defensive, unlike that for instance of the political demonstrator,
who chooses to attack.

The second sphere is of organization. Weber argued that
bureaucracy was the form of organization most suited to modern
economic needs. Many critics have pointed out that bureaucracies,
whilst they do allow an unmatched scale of rational control over
economic processes, often suffer from inflexibilities that reduce
their efficiency. To take a contemporary example: the planning
authority for the projected Australian town of Albury-Wodonga has
a chart that completely determines its tasks over an eighteen-month
period. This is irrational, in terms of authority's own goals (the
creation of an attractive, well-functioning city), and exhibits the
same trait of an excessive need for control, for rigidity, coupled with
an exaggerated fear of disruption, which I have identified as
paranoid. Positivist thought and its institutional embodiment,
bureaucracy, are funded psychologically by motives that without
great magnification manifest themselves as paranoid. Where they
have managed to operate short of the threshold of pathology they
have made possible an unprecedented degree of control over
material reality; where, however, they have transgressed that
threshold, control has become a cage.

Another example of this drive for control turning paranoid is
provided by the cases of some leading Victorian intellectuals.
Carlyle, Matthew Arnold, Mill and Kingsley all suffered from

anxiety about purpose. They attempted to cope with their failing Puritanism by casting themselves as earnest exhortatory moralists, mounting ideologies of individualism, hero-worship, force and even commerce. Theirs was precisely the priestly moralism that Nietzsche isolated as the canker of the age. Their works do ring hollow today, lacking psychological depth. These Victorians in their search for assurance attempted to substitute the false security of dogma for the genuine culture that works with the uncertain ebb and flow of inner drives. Here are the Puritans for whom authority failed, at one remove, one step down the road to remission.

Other manifestations of paranoia might readily be instanced. We might note, for example, the current success of catastrophe films. The length of box office queues in the USA, Britain and Australia indicate that no other media fads could compete in 1975 with those that catalysed Armageddon fantasies. It is the same deep insecurity at the root of paranoid defences that is exploited and compelled by these fictions of sudden and total disaster, in which earthquake, fire or bomb devastates the womb-like security of the ship, the airliner or the skyscraper. (This craze is reminiscent of that for invasion novels in late Victorian and Edwardian England.)

(My historical model is not one of simple linear cultural change. The transition from Puritan to remissive is a trend, which runs through a continuous progression of cycles. The model is analogous to the economist's representation of the trade cycle through time. For example, the influence of 'counter-culture' ideology over university students appears to have declined from its peak, and we are currently experiencing a return to a more industrious, Puritan orientation to academic studies. But this will be temporary, and even in the low bend of the cycle it is merely quasi-Puritan.)

I wish, finally, to take up an inference to be drawn from the third chapter, on the remissive, that the paranoid may have become a more integral part of our culture than is suggested by placing it circumscriptly as a product of a testing rapids in an evolutionary current. Freud argued that repressed destructiveness transforms into guilt. This is Meursault's case. The hedonist ideology of today, in its monistic utopianism, cannot recognize destructive emotions; it will ensure that the remissive's superego polices their repression. Consequently, augmenting guilt is inevitable in post-Puritan culture, that is if we accept Freud's later view that aggression is innate, or at least so prevalent in Western history, and manifest from the individual's first year of life, that the more correct assumption is that it is innate.

I suggested earlier that the psychic turbulence experienced in the rapids separating Puritan from remissive allows four possible responses. Those of the conservative and the Puritan-remissive are not at this point problematic. But the responses of the dominant two bear closer scrutiny: the paranoid and the remissive-hedonist are victims of a vicious circle of accumulating guilt, which for ideological reasons cannot be recognized and thereby accumulates further. For the paranoid, paranoia breeds paranoia, guilt exploding periodically as futile and angry moralism. For his remissive-hedonist brother, the psychological dynamics are no easier: he has no outlet at all, unless he can rationalize it as remission. Indeed, the very commitment to hedonism will generate strains that increase the remissive task, release now being required both from the Puritan past and its lodged character, and from tensions set up by those new norms that themselves establish release as a goal. This is a crippling ambivalence, and it ensures that no fully remitted personality will ever emerge: the remissive-hedonist reality is the enfeebled, undionysian child of current flux. It is a commonplace of psychoanalysis that a consequence of repressed hostile impulses, forced inwards against the ego, is depression.

There is another factor compounding personal malaise. Puritan culture had its way of coping with guilt: sublimating it through vocation. Now that the bourgeois achievement ethic is in disrepute, the self-flagellant has lost his whip, his method of release which, learned over generations, brought him some measure of secure well-being. New modes of release cannot be satisfactorily tailored overnight, and in the interim of disorientation waves of intense anxiety are likely - as already suggested this situation is conducive to paranoia. Psychological unemployment may be the severest ill resulting from the withering of the Puritan work drive. (Changes come slowly. Recent sociology shows the enduring centrality in Britain and America of a man's work to his sense of purpose. It is usually not that the work is particularly satisfying in itself; it is sustained rather by the fantasy the individual has about its communal significance, about the opportunity it provides him for challenge, career and advancement, and about the important place it earns him in his own family. Maybe the growing incidence of household neurosis indicates that no equivalent fantasy supports the often more varied and interesting tasks of keeping a house and children. What is indicated is that men will experience rising levels of nervousness themselves as their work fantasy fades.)

Finally, the remissive is by constitution hostile to forms. Form spells constraint. But just as the remissive himself depends on norms, a fact he prefers to deny, his society is like any other in needing forms to protect it from its own incipient nihilism. The attack on forms is deluded: conceived of as removing the limits to pleasure, it rather abolishes the foundations of security. The attack carries in its misreading of reality a symptom of paranoia. Genuine outbreaks of paranoia are likely to follow, as the anxiety and guilt intensified by the anomic consequences of the elimination of forms seek outlet, channelled as moral indignation.

So the paranoid and the remissive emerge now as two parallel, sometimes alternative, sometimes conjoined strategies for coping with the same problem: how to live with Puritan dispositions once the supporting culture has been flattened. Our opening conjecture that they rather represent styles of behaviour that are historically consecutive on the continuum of cultural evolution moves into the background. Whereas the paranoid does precede the remissive, preparing its way, it does not then itself lapse, its task completed. It has a role of its own in post-Puritan culture; the new psychological milieu is conducive to the breeding of paranoids. The langour of the remissive-hedonist, at his feeblest, severed from the succouring past, groping for a delusory future, like a dying kitten, is functionally equivalent to the distorted perceptions and the unrealistic emotional responses of the paranoid.

6

The Remissive Prospect

A sociology of culture, like any human or social science, in the fact that its explanations largely assume causal form, must take seriously problems of origin and account for a significant length of their infinite regress. Only by tracing back a few elements in the series may a clue to its deeper formula be revealed. In the particular case of the Puritan, the paranoid and the remissive we can fairly claim that the first causal step has been taken: a description of the cultural change, spelt out in terms of its manifestations in different areas of human thought and action, providing an account of the psychological dynamic at work. But a second step is also vital and it involves answering the question of what began the shift, what provoked the decline of Puritan culture and ensured that it would move in a remissive direction. I would be contented with the rudiments of an answer, for a precise and comprehensive reply would require coping not only with the infinite detail of relevant periods, but also with the infinite historical regress, back step by step to the Reformation, and beyond, to Adam and Eve, and then even into geophysics and astronomy.

I have made some suggestions about what has lain behind the change from Puritan to remissive. An affinity was interpreted linking major changes in economic conditions, in the domains of production and consumption, with the rise of remissive culture. Economic institutions have some degree of self-determination, of independence from other factors; they thus constitute one causal influence. Technological advances have, additionally, made possible the modern mass media and a multitude of leisure aids, thereby furthering the remissive. Other spheres of human activity, such as knowledge and art, also develop with a degree of autonomy, that is, obeying in part an internal logic. Accordingly, for instance, the secularizing impact of the Enlightenment, followed by the evolution of Romanticism, and then psychology, must have made its own causal contribution to the cultural change we have been investigating.

At a more abstract level there is the intangible vitalist factor that Henri Pirenne took as formative in each stage of European history. Barbarian tribes, societies, cultures, epochs or whatever have a limited amount of energy; they rise with great forging thrust, for a few generations move conquering all in their path, then slowly expire, as if inwardly exhausted. If this metaphor has validity then the surprise in our case is that Puritan culture lasted so long, and that it was so successful in incorporating new elements as the old withered.

Here I feel it pointless to go further. I am not confident that much progress will ever be made in this very general area, and prefer myself to withdraw back to the context of my descriptions and to finish by trying to close them off.

The question remains as to whether a remissive/paranoid society is viable. The tradition in political theory that includes Machiavelli, Hobbes, Hume, Burke, Tocqueville, Durkheim, Weber and finally Freud holds that social stability is dependent on the effective sanctioning of norms which constrain the egoistic impulses of individuals. The question follows: will a culture be viable in which no public constraints are placed upon the individual apart from those technological rigidities caused by either the pressures of limited resources or the delays of gestation periods of adaption to new social needs? This is a question about authority, about whether a social order in which authority is the preserve of economic institutions, and then in the implicit form of the controlling existence of the industrial state, which is in turn governed by its own inherent capacities and inflexibilities, will be able to satisfy the surplus impulses of its myriad subjects. More particularly we are asking what forms and what degree of individual obedience will be necessary for such a social order to maintain itself.

There have been predictions about what a remissive culture will entail, ranging from the bleak nihilism of Nietzsche's 'death of god' and Dostoevsky's 'all things are permitted', projections of a society in which the decline of individual authority renders personal and social experience gratuitous, to the contemporary utopian view that the end of the interim phase of paranoia has produced the first of a new generation, able to do without authority, untrammelled by social pressures, playfully anarchically gay. The first step towards clarifying this field is to recapitulate on the different character-types that it now seems will be prominent in a maturely remissive culture. There are four of these character-types.

First, *remissive-hedonist man*. He has gained some remission from the cardinal sins of his fathers and lives in some proximity to his hedonist ideal, pleasure-oriented but undionysian. However, he shows signs of tending through time to his alter ego - the *nihilist-depressive*. Nietzsche prophesied that the erosion of faith in absolutes would lead an élite few to concentrate on the self as a surrogate god, but had as its ultimate point nihilism of the depressive mode. This would not be the world of the Russian nihilists, but of Baudelaire's ennui, of *fin de siècle* cynicism, of life which is prototypically secular, and bored, experienced in a context lacking hierarchy or moral imperative. The psycho-historical stage in which the individual achieves his zenith, finding nothing apart from himself of interest, the stage of psychological man, prepares the way to the last door, through which even the self loses its command. Psychoanalysis, as a training in detachment from neurotic absorptions, is in danger of catalysing a generalized state of indifference.

Second, the *paranoid*. His most common guise will be that of the *nihilist-delinquent*. The decline of authority means, in terms of individual psychology, the elimination of the role of the father-figure and consequently the failure fully to internalize moral systems, to develop conscience. A fatherless society produces the nihilist as its black sheep. But nihilism develops two variants, of which the first, the depressive, is socially harmless, at the worst requiring hospitalization. The second variant is delinquent, Dostoevsky's gratuitously violent criminal for whom everything is permitted because he does not believe in either God or derivative constraints. This is not the nihilism of Nechaev, who pursued the revolutionary ideal, or of Hitler, who was driven by a curious blend of megalomanic racialist-nationalist idealism. It produces rather the crime without authority, without economic or psychological motive: exemplar of this mode is the *Clockwork Orange* of Burgess and Kubrick. The remissive culture has peculiar difficulties in restraining delinquency: not wishing to employ the punitive techniques of the old culture, it seeks to devise a compromise prison-hospital. In fact, it would like to approve of all styles of personal expression, hence the paranoid transition in which delinquency is idealized and blame is directed against parents and their social context.

Third, the *visionary*. The demise of Puritan authority opens the way for a type whose devaluation or even eclipse of self is complemented by the instating of fantasy as the replacement god. Artaud asserted that the ego is a cage. Here pleasure is visionary ecstasy, whether it appears in the form of schizophrenic hallucination (Ophelia blasted with ecstasy), noumenal revelation (Luther's mystical union with God) or cosmological fantasy (Blake's visionary books or the futurist speculation of Kubrick's film *2001 - A Space Odyssey*). Presumably all societies have produced their visionaries. What is notable at present is the scale of renewed interest in the pleasure possibilities of pure fantasy. This interest has been facilitated by better knowledge of cultures that have devoted more attention to developing metaphysical pursuits, and in particular knowledge of their techniques of meditation, ritual and drug usage. The visionary's world is the most private of all, for the boundaries of the universe are contained within the horizons of his individual imagination. The schizophrenic is the limiting case. But nearly as acute is the social isolation of Carlos Castaneda's guru, of the Zen master, of Martin Heidegger in the mysticism of his late works, and of the characters in the novels of Patrick White - particularly those in his epic *Riders in the Chariot*.

Fourth and finally, *Puritan-remissive man*. This last of the great Puritan types, one of whose sterner exemplars was Freud himself, survives. Self-knowledge retains, in some milieux, authority: there, the individual remains fascinated by the subjective nuances of feeling and fantasy that he experiences. Puritan-remissive man is an aesthete of personality, seeking ever more sophisticated self-understandings. He conducts his remission within a strict framework of disciplined Puritan seriousness. His contemporary literary representatives are Robbe-Grillet, Rohmer (the film *Le Genou de Claire*), and Malle (the films *Le Souffle au Coeur* and *Lacombe Lucien*). They are paralleled in the field of academic psychology by Klein, Fairbairn, Erikson and their followers - although in the quality of their work, or in the stature of the guiding personality, there has been no match for Freud.

The viability of the remissive culture will depend on which

character-types become predominant, and whether conflicts between their desires and the needs of the framing technocracy will remain at tolerable levels. Phases of paranoia are more likely to be superficially disruptive than revolutionary, generating tensions that can be accommodated without marked structural change. If the nihilist-delinquent becomes prevalent, he will probably force a return to punishing restraints, but with the increasingly remissive bias of treatment by drugs and psychological conditioning. Here, as elsewhere, when authority is required it will come in the form of technology and social engineering and not individual presence.

The visionary is largely irrelevant to this question. The incidence of violent psychosis may well increase, but although its manifestations will be startling (political assassination, the Manson murders, the attack on Michaelangelo's *Pietà*), they will be readily containable by the expansion of the prison-hospital and the innovation of suitable therapeutic techniques. Moreover, the degree to which remissive-hedonist everyman indulges in drug-induced hallucination will most likely be governed by the technocracy, by the degree to which it can do without his work-services - personal income, as the means to consumer satisfaction, will remain for most a definitive sanction against letting the industrial state run down.

The case of Puritan-remissive man is also unlikely to be relevant to this question. Although his is the single style appropriate to a modern Puritan disposition, the probability is low that he will continue to exert any marked public influence. To be sure, the roots of some Puritan characters may survive the constant pressure towards remissive adaptation; their securing attachments to the values of perfection, discipline and responsibility may resist erosion with each new generation. But they will face a hostile public domain, economically geared to servicing the remissive-hedonist natures on whom it will bestow exclusive legitimacy. These last Puritans are certain to be relegated to the social provinces of deviancy. We may well be witnessing in the continued presence of Puritan-remissive man, as we do in Robbe-Grillet's novels and films, the last gasp of the long European cultural tradition. At the most he will maintain a small, marginal, although possibly widely respected élite.

Thus the issue of viability lies in the court of remissive-hedonist man himself. Assuming that his will be the dominating presence in a remissive culture, apart from cycles of delinquent outbursts, two questions must be asked. First, will science be able to fund the continued technological ingenuity that the industrial state will require if it is to survive? The genesis myth, in its assertion that man's primal crime was to seek after knowledge, determined that *homo sapiens* would thereafter live by the assumption that the way to redeem his fall was through the pursuit of further knowledge. One of the few areas in which this assumption has appeared to be vindicated is the application of technology to cure the ills created by technology.

With regard to knowledge itself, the administration of the industrial state will depend on the survival of positivist methods. Moreover, research scientists will need more Puritan self-discipline than in the past to reach a level of competence equal to solving the problems created by man's proliferating needs and his continual disruption of his relationship to nature. Creative science has always been the preserve of fanatical and eccentric individuals: whether their counterparts in the future will be corrupted from their ascetic calling by the hedonism of remissive man will be a crucial question for the survival of Western civilization. Indeed, my entire argument about the rise of remissive culture assumes the survival of a relatively stable economic base; it assumes that the last ton of fossilized coal, or some substitute, will not be used up, and that the West will not disappear in a cataclysm of pollution, radio-active or otherwise.

The second question relevant to the emerging society's viability concerns the non-scientist, non-expert majority, and whether their lives will work for or against the unfolding order of remissive culture and its technological infrastructure. The nihilist-depressive will present a threat to social viability if he becomes so prevalent as to create a situation of Spenglerian decadence, with resources of human vitality too low to cope with problems of external danger or internal disharmony. The majority will never be completely divested of a serious social role; at the least it is they who provide the children from whose number the next generation of engineers must come. Then there is the allied question of whether resentment against an order that is seen to have killed possibilities for human fulfilment, that has nurtured a style of social life flagrantly at odds with prevailing hedonist ideology, resentment asserted in disruption at work, vandalism at play, hostility to any innovative project, rancour at any authority, will neutralize already depleted reserves of energy for generating purposive social movement. The question is whether psychological depression will be projected into economic depression, whether the individual remissive's unconscious masochistic wish will be worked out publicly as social disintegration.

These questions are, necessarily, today, unanswerable. As always, the owl of Minerva may take flight only at dusk. Let us hope that Goethe's dictum, that sadly we come to live out in middle age the fantasies of our youth, does not generalize beyond private life.

part 2

Footnotes

7

The New England Flight from Calvin: Some Sociological Impressions

The most puzzling question about Calvinism to a twentieth-century sociologist is how its harsh doctrines could ever have appealed to anyone. In general the function that a church and its commands fulfils for its members is that of making their world intelligible and providing them with assurance. Thus, in the century in which Christianity was most obviously withering, Carlyle observed that for him and his contemporaries, 'destitute of belief', the great attraction of Walter Scott's heroes was that they 'went forth in the most determined manner, nothing doubting'. Thomas Arnold described doubt as man's most grievous affliction.

But Calvin, while accepting that 'Satan's most grievous temptation is to unsettle men with doubt about their election', insisted that precisely because man was weak, and incommunicably remote from his God, he could never be assured of his own salvation. William Perkins would later assert, true to the spirit of Calvin's *Institutes*, that uncertainty itself was the surest earthly sign of a saint. Rather than founding a morality that would defend its faithful against anxiety and doubt, reinforce their sense of purpose and protect their community from anomie, Calvin demanded that men accept their worthlessness and ignorance and yet live as if they were chosen, as exemplars; he offered at best the flimsy, ambivalent counsel that the discomfort they suffered might itself be an index of virtue, and that they should not give in to their impulse to escape it. He was troubled himself, through his *Institutes*, about assurance, and liked to insist that men who have received saving grace, the Word, will know it, will be confident. But he was quick to dampen any 'sheer confidence' with the Pauline 'Let him who stands well, take heed lest he fall', and 'Be not proud but fear!' to which he added in his own blunt language, 'God can cut you off'.

Calvin's praise of doubt gained a practical dimension in his contrasting notions of the visible and the invisible church. God alone can recognize the chosen; he alone knows who belongs to the community of the elect, the invisible church. But those who aspired to godliness needed to meet together, for preaching and the administration of the sacraments, and for these purposes they formed a mundane, visible church. This latter church would include both good and evil men, saints and hypocrites; it would exclude only those who were obviously wicked. Pragmatic though Calvin was, accepting that no earthly institution could be perfect, his distinction reinforced the harshness of this theology, for no member of the visible church could ever be assured that he belonged to the all-important invisible one.

The most plausible response for anyone who accepted this chronic mode of fatalism, so undermining of human confidence, would be to renounce all earthly striving as futile. But Calvin asserted: 'Man, being taught that he has nothing good left in his possession, and being surrounded on every side with the most miserable necessity, should, nevertheless, be instructed to aspire to the good of which he is destitute.' He elsewhere declared that men are responsible for every exigency of life, except salvation. So, men are almost totally responsible, must accept almost total guilt, must remorselessly pursue their vocation of good works, and yet may draw no ultimate comfort or satisfaction from having lived with impeccable responsibility. Such a paradox could have taken practical root only where it articulated some dark, inescapable psychological schism. (The same schism finds illustration later, more abstractly, in free-will/determinism discussions, and, to take one twentieth-century example, in Camus's explication of Sisyphus as the paradigm for the human paradox of the purposive pursuit of absurd goals.)

Calvin was followed, in England and elsewhere, by Presbyterians in particular, but also by others. His doctrines were, however, by 1600 subject to a scrutiny that generated, if not explicit amendments, at least a sense that there were problems and contradictions in the original text that demanded answers. From the 1620s, a number of divines centred in Cambridge, notably Perkins, Ames, Preston and Sibbes, developed 'covenant theology', a reinterpretation of Calvin that served to lessen the distance between man and God by introducing the notion of illustration, that good works, while they do not contribute to salvation, provide an index for recognizing who is saved. Thus a man might take comfort from his diligent pursuit of vocation, for he had been allowed thereby to demonstrate his godliness, a sign that he was elect. Covenant theology, moving from an initial view that God established a covenant of grace with fallen man, comes finally to argue that a man may prepare himself, by right living, for the granting of grace; his virtue may attract God's good will. This theological endeavour to make God's will more visible, to allow men some assurance, shifted Calvinism closer to a works covenant, and the Arminian heresy that works save.

The question of what social conditions, what psychological disposition, led to men being drawn to pure Calvinism is vital to an understanding both of the specific complex of the rise of Protestantism and capitalism in Europe, and a range of general sociological problems about the links between asceticism and conduct, ideology and practice, belief and purpose. This question is also central to our whole understanding of culture. Weber quite rightly isolated it as the decisive empirical ground on which to explore the origins of modern European society; but by taking the religious factor as causal he avoided the question of how that factor itself took root, a question that subsequent scholarship has advanced, but not very successfully, in the main merely reversing, or half-reversing the causal link, taking capitalism as principal.

In this essay I wish to take up the related but smaller and more accessible question of the dissolution of pure Calvinism in the particular case of Boston during that colony's first decades. The volume and quality of scholarly material on the founding of Massachusetts makes this a unique historical context in which to ask some sociological questions about Puritanism.

As Massachusetts was being founded in the 1620s and 1630s, theological change was in the air. But the new ideas were more than simply taken up in the new colony; they were applied in a progressively more extreme form. I am interested here in why Calvinism should have been radically revised in this case, in which it played the role of guiding ideology in the creation from nothing of a living church and a living community.

John Cotton was one of the few in Boston in the formative 1630s who held fairly strictly to Calvin's teachings, stressing grace rather than works, arguing for a recognition of self-contained,

introspective individualism in spiritual affairs by a church that at the
same time was an integral community of men working together
under an earthly covenant. This Calvinist balance which Cotton
defended would be a precarious achievement under any social
circumstances. In the infant colony it was vulnerable on the one side
to those like Anne Hutchinson and her followers, who slanted
Cotton's teachings into a kind of sectarian mysticism, regarding
themselves as saints among the damned, Antinomian, and as such
hostile to the practical needs of a community groping to establish a
sense of its own coherency and viability. Significantly, the section of
this militant group which moved to Narragansett Bay, after Boston
had excommunicated it, was plagued by difficulties of its own in
creating worldly community; its attempt to found a theocracy soon
split into antagonistic sects, one at Portsmouth, the other at
Newport.

Cotton's balance was more profoundly vulnerable, however,
from the other side, to those who wanted a more tangible, visible
religion, Thomases who needed to feel the stigmata. These men
were like those early Christians who had sought in pagan ritual a
palliative to ease the burdens of monotheistic religion; men who
quite simply sought a religion that offered them assurance.

A society that felt the need to expel an Anne Hutchinson as a
threat to its stability, would, out of the same insecurity about its
own capacities for surviving the tensions generated by dissidence in
its midst, demand that virtue and vice be visible. Boston's first
minister, John Wilson, called from the pulpit for personal
reformation, a coming closer to God through godly conduct; he
emphasized works rather than grace. He continued the move of
covenant theology to narrow the distance between man and God.
The slow and steady erosion of Calvinist harshness produced a
conflict which manifested itself in Boston in 1636 in theological
debate. The Reverend Thomas Shepard attacked Cotton, the
Boston church's 'teacher', for failing to understand that a church
must be founded upon a visible morality. His case, as Rutman
paraphrases it, argued that:

> To stress to such an extent the personal quest for evidence of
> God's grace, to dismiss the ordinances of the church as
> comforting but ineffectual, to preach God's spirit rather than the
> moral law, absolute faith rather than conduct, was to unleash an
> individual approach to God undermining all formal religion.

Calvinism here panics at its central contradiction, the contradiction that both articulates and stimulates the tensions that endow the Puritan character with its dynamism; Calvinism here is no longer confident enough to carry its own formative burden. Although Wilson and Shepard themselves did not quite reach the point of claiming that a man gains benefit from good works, they had watered the seed of Arminianism, whose more comfortable doctrine of election would eventually flourish into predominance in New World Puritanism. They had, more immediately, contributed to the New England innovation, the notion of visible sainthood, which rationalized their earthly church as the exclusive congregation of the elect, with a monopoly of virtue.

Historians are not completely decided on the sequence of events that led to the adoption in New England of the Congregationalist model for church organization, with its insistence on the examination of intending members to ensure that they both understood the scriptures and had received saving faith, and thus could demonstrate that they were among the elect. Boston's founding governor, John Winthrop, would have been familiar in England with the theory of Congregationalism; moreover, he was confronted by its practice when his ship first landed, at the already established settlement of Salem. Some explanation for the move away from the less rigid Presbyterian model is to be found in the fact that it would have been the most intolerant, least flexible of Puritans who left England, ones who were incensed to extremes by mounting hostility towards their religion, or alternatively ones like the Pilgrims who may have left their adopted home, Leyden in Holland, partly because it was too tolerant a community, too eclectic for their strict tastes. This type of migrant would by disposition be attracted to a more authoritarian and legalistic church order. But it is two other factors that I am most interested in.

Functional as it was to the well-being of the individual, the revised doctrine was functional to that of the community. Shepard's case is sociologically persuasive. Established English society, stabilized by traditions, could afford the luxury of maintaining dissident radicals on its margins. But when those radicals transplanted themselves into a virgin situation, in which all basic social needs from building houses to framing laws had to be addressed, their idealism had to face practical tests. Puritan ideology had to be adapted to the routine daily problems that any community must solve merely in order to survive. Above all, the viability of the early settlements was dependent upon a sense of collective faith, of communal purpose, upon a higher and universal goal that would both bind individuals together in spite of their personal differences, and carry them through times of despair provoked by the enormity of their pioneering task. Crucially that element in their religion that devalued social sanction, stressing that virtue was a private matter between the individual and his conscience, had to be reduced, and for the reason Shepard advanced.

Further, only in this manner could a social hierarchy be consolidated whose own authority was reinforced by religious authority. If sainthood were visible, then the chosen ones could form a homogenous and exclusive élite with the power to decide both who was eligible to enter the church congregation, and conversely whom amongst the pariahs should be indicted under state law for their transgressions. The suppression of Calvin's doubt made possible the more consistent implementing of a social process for assessing sin, whereby the good sat in courts and administered prisons so that the fallen might be rightfully punished. Freud's conviction was that the main function of punishment is to improve the punisher, thus appeasing *his* doubt. The neo-Calvinist amalgamation of church and state made available a form peculiarly suitable for confirming the self-righteousness of the élite.

Any established society has complex roots, which endow it with an innate stability, an image of validity by virtue of thereness, and techniques for accommodating strains from within and without, all of which make it normally more tolerant of diversity than a new foundation. But there is also a psychological factor governing acts of uprooting. Men who break free from the society that has fostered them live out a fantasy of parricide, and thereby subject themselves to the guilt of the ambivalent son, who destroys what he both hates and at the same time depends upon: guilt fed by the double threat that he has destroyed all authority, and hence rendered the world void, indifferent, anomic, and that he has himself taken on the envied authority of the father, taken his place, and is now vulnerable to the identical syndrome of assassination by his own sons/followers/subjects. The prodigal son must return home for blessing before he can legitimately start out alone, if he ever can. To truly settle and build afresh, the settler must have paid off all his debts in his old world. It follows that the fathers of a new community will desperately need assurance of their right to have done what they have, and to go on; they will likely, except in unusual cases, of which John Winthrop seems to have been one, be drawn to authoritarian institutions and authoritarian ideology (to protect them from their sons, and from what is much the same, their own latent guilt). Many men in this situation are driven to recreate what they have destroyed, rebuild the old world brick by brick in the new. (This parricide syndrome does not however fit the merchant, who is not necessarily a rebel; he usually mediates old and new worlds, at a mercantile distance from the authority of either.)

The settlers bore not only the practical strains of having to construct a society from scratch, of surviving the first winter; they also had private demons to counter. Such demons would not, however, rest once the new order was founded. The pure Calvinist doctrine instructed the settler that whilst he had achieved good works by managing to build a civilization in the wilderness, and in that he could take some pride, these works would neither help nor hinder his progress in God's eyes. The catharsis of fulfilled vocation might ameliorate doubt; but for Calvin not even that was an ultimate gain. Now the parricide discovers that guilt is renewed by success: he has achieved what was forbidden to him, built his own graven image. Calvinist ideology in its own ambivalence to this-worldly success offered him some symbolic representation for his psychological state, and in that would have provided some relief from strain. But it reinforced rather than lessened doubt and gave it some legitimacy. Moreover, this ideology did not include parricidal images; if anything, to the contrary, it stressed the intractability of authority. (Milton filled this cultural gap with his parricidal Satan, painting the archetypal rebellion in heroic colours.) There was therefore much to recommend to the pilgrim in the wilderness a rewriting of the theological canon, a rewriting that would grant him the support, the affirmation, of being able to claim his good works as an index of virtue, even a contribution towards it, and to be able to claim before his community that he had incontrovertible evidence of his own salvation. Increasing the visibility of virtue meant increasing the individual's sense of control and, conversely, lessening the threat of nihilism. As a result of these accommodations, the original ambivalence to parricide must have reasserted itself, in pride at having succeeded in the practical world, now rationalized by religious dogma, and in guilt following from that very achievement. But this ambivalence would have proved to be a gain for the individual over the situation in which guilt alone was predominant.

To sum up: the strict Calvinist doctrine of election, and its focal ambivalence concerning doubt, would be difficult to live by under any circumstances. For the New England settlers, facing the extraordinary psychological challenge of founding a viable society in the wilderness, it was intolerable. They harnessed their guilt by setting up more authoritarian institutions than those they had left, and by committing themselves to a more rigid theology. That this guilt had been funded from capital drawn from conflicts over authority, legitimacy, rebellion and even regicide meant that the settlers would be condemned to repay their debt in the New World in the same psychological currency, setting up more punitive authorities, further reducing their own tolerance for uncertainty. There were exceptions, like the more pragmatic and tolerant Winthrop, or the Calvinist intellectual Cotton, but their vision was not to hold sway.

8

Puritan Character and
The Scarlet Letter

The Scarlet Letter is a love story. It is also a tale of sin and shame. These are necessary but preliminary observations. What is peculiar about its central moral concerns is their Puritan nature, that passion's distinctive form here is psychologically Puritan. My interest in this brief excursus is to take Hawthorne's two main characters, Hester Prynne and Arthur Dimmesdale, as case-studies for my Puritan type. I am not concerned with other questions of genre, nor with discussing the novel's technical quality. I will argue, by implication, that the work's appeal depends on the survival of the Puritan variant of the tradition of ascetic romance in the West.

The Scarlet Letter illustrates the tension in the New World, specifically for the second generation of Boston's settlers, between the revised doctrine of visible election and the orthodox Calvinist-Puritan doctrine which had stressed that even those who might consider themselves chosen are doomed to doubt, that in effect they too suffered from guilt that was essentially unredeemable. Hawthorne, in his novel, gives authorial blessing to the harsher original doctrine, and thereby to the classical Puritan character type. The parable to be read in Arthur Dimmesdale's death is that 'we are all sinners alike'; no one in the community is pure. Although Hester's girlhood is described as stainless, this is the more to stress that she is the single truly virtuous figure in the story. But she is the moral exemplar not because she is free from guilt; on the contrary, Hawthorne's psychology has as its pivot the ambivalence that 'there was the taint of deepest sin in the most sacred quality of human life'. Hester is among the elect because of the way she sublimates her guilt.

According to Milton, slanting Genesis, Adam's fall was due to love, love for woman. So it is for Hester Prynne. Hester's vocation is to love, and concurrently to do penance for that love which is sinful. Guilt and love harmoniously intertwine as her passion, which she plays out in her needlework, her craft at which she is a master, and which is the signature of her penance, her humble works for the rich and for the needy of the community. The ambivalence of love and of guilt is symbolized in her craft. She celebrates her love in 'gorgeously beautiful, voluptuous, Oriental, exquisite productions of her needle', such as the clothes in which she dresses her daughter; at the same time she does penance for her guilt by devoting much of her time to making coarse garments for the poor. In her craft she sublimates both a love beyond consummation and a guilt beneath penitence. But, of course, she does consummate her love in her own characteristically Puritan manner, as vocation. This ambivalence is represented further in what Hawthorne describes as the strange mixture of humility and pride with which she lives and works, testifying every moment before the unwitting community, which mistakes penance for penitence, to the twin facts of her love and her fall.

Hester fulfils the five criteria defining the Puritan. She does not regret: she does not expect, except for one short interlude, to be redeemed - she soon puts the momentarily discarded scarlet letter, emblem of her passion, back on again. She does not want her passion to wane, for that is what she lives by. Her passion is a private matter: she does penance for herself, because she herself believes she has sinned. It is secondary that she has also contravened public morality, and must publicly humble herself for that. The community merely provides a venue and a means for her essentially private devotional penance; she lives on its margins, in a cottage by herself, never seeking to compromise her solitude. Hawthorne, in alluding to her turn inwards, her meditativeness, her introspectiveness, stresses that society is only superficially significant to her: 'It is remarkable, that persons who speculate the most boldly often conform with the most perfect quietude to the external regulations of society.'

Hester could have left this apparently punitive environment. The two reasons that keep her are independent of any social constraint. First, there is the chain of her guilt, which could never be broken. Hawthorne writes in *The Scarlet Letter* of

a fatality, a feeling so irresistable and inevitable that it has the force of doom, which almost invariably compels human beings to linger around and haunt, ghost-like, the spot where some great and marked event has given the colour to their lifetime; and still more irresistably, the darker the tinge that saddens it.

Second, she stays because her companion in passion, to whom she is chained by 'the iron links of mutual crime', and of love, is there. After his death she leaves, but later returns, a fact that further illustrates the authority over her actions of the central ambivalence in her character.

Hester, finally, obeys the canon of honesty. The one act in her life that remains morally doubtful to her, her marriage to Chillingworth, is largely exonerated because she did not feign love: she made her feelings perfectly clear to him. She is free from either laziness or hypocrisy, the leading Puritan vices.

Hester is the paradigm Puritan in the orthodox Calvinist sense, represented in the New World by the teachings of John Cotton. She is the only figure in the novel chosen for divine favour. She is the one who lives by the Puritan code, and she gains a dignity from the singlemindedness of her devotion that even her fellow citizens recognize. Her favoured state as a Puritan has as its leading confirmation, in Hawthorne's judgment, the reiterated statement that her passion and its penance gave her, first, a kind of sacredness which enabled her to walk securely amid all peril; second, it provided her with a passport into regions where other women dared not tread; and third it gave her a sympathetic knowledge of the hidden sin in other hearts, it disciplined her to truth: 'Shame, Despair, Solitude! These had been her teachers. . . .' The unique understanding of the human heart that she is granted stands as a vindication of the manner in which she has conducted her passion. There is even a qualified redemption in the concluding picture of her living out her days in her cottage giving counsel to those drawn to her with their sorrows and perplexities. We are permitted to imagine Hester as having gained some serenity. Indeed, as Milton hoped, a Puritan may attain a higher state of being in the wisdom gained from measuring up to his passion and his guilt, not shrinking from it, in the manner in which he is called.

The Reverend Arthur Dimmesdale, who has also committed the sin of adultery, is appalled, as Hester is not, that he does not regret, appalled that he still loves and therefore still sins. For him expiation is rendered vain. His personal conflict is explicit in Puritan terms: his vocation as preacher, and thus as the community's moral example and guardian, is in opposition to his passion. He is guilty, consequently, of a second sin, hypocrisy. Nevertheless, there is a kind of synthesis in that it is precisely his guilt about his love that causes him the anguish which infuses his sermons with their magical, charismatic quality. His gift, his 'tongue of fire', his divinely inspiring presence, lives off his devotional penance; and indeed his sermons are but thinly disguised confessions of his crime. His vocation, at which he too has achieved mastery, functions as a sublimation and attains its finest exposition after his final full recognition that he continues to love: 'Never had man spoken in so wise, so high, and so holy a spirit.' But the hypocrisy of his position is by now intolerable to him; and the strength from his love at last gives him the thrust to speak his conscience in public.

Arthur's tragedy, however, is more than one precipitated by a split passion. Arthur is not a Puritan of quite the same mould as Hester. While he does finally recognize that all men are sinners, this is a painful and defeated acceptance, and suggests that he has been living an easier, more utopian doctrine of election, holding that sinlessness is possible, or at least that guilt can be expiated. This explains why he should be so disturbed that he, the Boston community's moral exemplar, is not pure. In effect he disregards the third Puritan criterion, that guilt is irredeemably cumulative. At the same time, he lives independently of the second, that salvation is a private matter between an individual and his God. Although he does once cry out to Roger Chillingworth, 'But who art thou that dares thrust himself between the sufferer and his God?' his driving belief is that a man's conscience must be publicly exhibited. That Arthur is tormented by the sin of hypocrisy indicates his need for public confession, that for him private recognition is inadequate; he requires to be sinless in the eyes of the community. His Puritan commitment to self-honesty forbids him his vocation, preaching against sin, unless ideally he is without sin himself, or at worst unless he is stringently honest with the public in the baring of his own soul. Even his one attempt to rationalize his situation draws on the easier doctrine of election: he suggests to Chillingworth that it may be better for a man to keep his blackness secret so that he can continue to work in the world, and save the chance to gain redemption through better service. Here he verges on the Arminian heresy, abhorred by an earlier generation of Puritans, and in particular on its doctrine that a man can influence his own salvation by means of will. Arthur is Puritan by disposition, there is no escape for him personally from his passion/guilt; it is existentially binding, and his Puritan self-honesty forces him to recognize the attendant impossibility of penitence and therefore of redemption. At the same time, he yokes himself to the neo-Calvinist ideology taken up by his fellow citizens in Boston, which by decreeing that the godly are the unstained does not permit him his vocation as preacher unless he is pure himself. By the first code his anxiety and his doubt are indices of virtue, as is the exemplary preaching that they produce; by the second code that preaching is itself false, because the preacher has sinned.

Hawthorne's romance stands also as a Puritan parable in the domain of eros. While Puritanism permitted sensuality within marriage, or within what it viewed as the key relationship in a man's life, it emphasized the basis of that union as one of friendship, of working partnership, of the mutual pursuit of independent vocations. There is a strong ascetic current here, a positing of high levels of instinctual renunciation, of self-control, of rationality and of disciplined work as indispensable to viable relationship. This ascetic psychology underpins *The Scarlet Letter*: Hester and Arthur never live together - indeed the compatibility for life of the temperamentally frail preacher and the woman of inner fortitude in other terms than the ones they live is questionable. But whether or not they spend the hours of daily existence together is immaterial: the successful pursuit of their separate vocations is what governs their sanity, and ensures that their passion endures. For the Puritan, culture, one of whose components is the art of human relationship, is the product of the sublimation of impulses that are deeply sunk in the bedrock of character where their potential force and their potential for working either good or evil remains unknown; the prospect of any but devious, scrupulously controlled release terrifies; these impulses threaten, if freed openly, to exhaust the housing personality, and shatter that delicately complex superstructure of symbol and act that forms Puritan life and enables its own peculiar logic of gratification.

Hawthorne's tale pivots psychologically on this view that love as passion, and guilt as passion, are mutually infusing and mutually

indispensable. The intense sensuality that colours the meeting of
Hester and Arthur in the forest has an extraordinary vividness
because it is the transmutation of a life-time of accumulated
renunciation, culpability, enforced control and distance. Intimacy's
key here is distance. The relationship endures, and with an
intensity, a clarity, and an absorption which discloses the austere,
severe material from which it was painfully woven. We are
confronted with the dialectic, familiar since the eleventh century in
the West, of ascetic love, the dialectic of prohibition and catharsis.

The work of modern scholars such as Perry Miller and Edmund
Morgan suggests that Hawthorne's picture of mid-seventeenth-
century Boston was fairly accurate. Rutman's work would imply that
if there was any flaw it was in showing the town more pious and less
mercantile than it was in reality. The easier doctrine of election
taken up in the New World, positing that salvation on earth is
visibly available, contravened the second Puritan criterion, that a
man's redemption is primarily his own concern. In shifting
emphasis from private virtue to public gesture it cancelled the
founding rationale for ascetic Puritanism. As Hawthorne illustrates
in his portrait of the Puritan community of *The Scarlet Letter*, it
thereby served to breed hypocrisy. Moreover, this shift of emphasis,
by effectively separating public virtue off from private deviancy,
removed the significance of vocation, of the individual working
publicly to illustrate his personal salvation.

Hawthorne's Boston citizens in their visible sainthood are
complacent and without true vocation. Hester could not have borne
her passion without a vocation to articulate it; conversely, where
there is no passion there can be no vocation. The citizens
consequently live without experiencing their innermost Puritan
core. Strong mediation between public and private is the more
important for the true Puritan because of the distance he strives to
maintain; without vocation he has no means for working out his
fantasies in public; without vocation the private can only be
repressed.

The most striking cautionary tale in the novel, however, is that of
Roger Chillingworth, the man who lived as a scholar but discovered
his true vocation was elsewhere when he met Hester. The passion
and vocation he then goes in search of eludes him and he fastens in
compensation like a 'leech' (Hawthorne's image) on those who have

found their deeper momentum. He is increasingly consumed by rancour, a type of inverted passion, which in the end destroys him. In the moral categories that the novel develops, Chillingworth becomes the pure image of evil balancing the flawless good towards which Hester and Arthur move; he is their satanic double.

In terms of the tension in New England Puritanism between personal salvation and viable community, Arthur is the more interesting of Hawthorne's two leading characters. Hester is representative of that type of Puritanism attacked by Shepard as dangerously individualistic. The quality of her personal destiny might go hand in hand with not only the degradation but the dissolution of community. While it is significant to her well-being that she can parade her sin in the form of her penance in public, there is a pride in this, and she does not care deeply what her fellow citizens think or know of her - she has no qualms about keeping secret the identity of her lover. Her first commitment is to her passion and this fortunately involves no conflict with her vocation. Her private needs are congruent with the demands the public places upon her. Consequently she does not have explicit moral problems: she is aware of what she has done, she is aware that she does not regret, and she is psychologically capable of accepting the consequences.

Arthur, however, must confess publicly; he is bound by community norms. He is an individual whose nature is in conflict with public demands, a conflict that is neatly illustrated at the level of ideology by the contradictoriness of the original Puritan doctrine of election and its weaker form. This is not a simple dualism, between the isolated Romantic individual and an unambiguously repressive society, for Arthur's private fulfilment is dependent on more than the pursuit of private passion, his love for Hester; his well-being depends also on his ability and opportunity to pursue his vocation. It follows that even if he had managed to live coherently by the original doctrine he still would have had to face the social problem, although it may not have as deeply troubled his conscience, that he might successfully fulfil his vocation only as long as his private life remained secret.

Seventeenth-century Puritan communities viewed no vocation more highly than that of preacher. Arthur had an unequalled responsibility for the community's sense of its own legitimacy. His sermons were the kindling that kept the collective conscience flaming. The exemplary conduct of his vocation was as indispensable to the lives of his fellow Bostonians as it was, in a different way, to his own. There was a further achievement, in that he managed to feed his preaching on the tensions of his private life, of his private meditations with his conscience, thus sublimating personal anguish for the communal good. His vocation successfully mediated private and public, infusing each with the logic of its complement. The cost of this enterprise was far higher in emotional currency than Hester's; and likewise the consequences for the town of its final breakdown must have been serious.

We are left with two variants of the Puritan type. Arthur's is the more instructive in its representation of the inevitable Puritan conflict between, on the one hand, private passion and conscience, and on the other, public vocation and responsibility. Hester's is the more exemplary for achieving a liveable synthesis.

9

On the Functions of Culture

There are, necessarily, social-psychological assumptions underlying the theory of culture that I am employing, ones that in an essay threaded to psychological ideal-types even more than otherwise need dragging out into the open, as far as that elusive labour is manageable. For instance, this question needs addressing: is my own analysis, which purports to be 'objective', wholly or partly conditioned by one of the types that it is aimed at explicating; is, say, my psychology in part a Puritan psychology and, therefore, a tool fashioned from the same crystal it is meant to cut? The first function of culture asserted above, Simmel's, assumes a notion of innate disposition, and the centrality of the individual as a cultural entity - assumptions that smell of cultural relativity. Moreover, the very notion 'disposition' has been harnessed in this essay with the intention of explaining a great deal, but it has not itself been examined. If we are to be reduced to reductionism, let us at least get clear on what first cause we stand (those social scientists who casually attack their colleagues for reductionism would sound more convincing if they knew the grain of their own beam).
Culture's first function, I claimed, is

> to constitute the process of symbol formation and utilization by which the individual, obeying an indigenous drive, makes objectively actual his inner core of potential subjective perfection.

This appears to assume that there is an 'inner man', and that he is in some sense 'pre-cultural', or more precisely, that the individual has an essence that in the context of his own biography antecedes social influences. My intention, however, is to posit a weaker variant of the nature over nurture thesis, avoiding entering the maze of that debate. I am taking as my starting point the work of Freud and Klein which suggests that the main lines of character disposition are determined in, at the most extended period, the first few years of life. The social factor is thus important but of short duration, and restricted to the influence of one or two individuals, crucially the mother. I am extrapolating further that however psychologically knowledgeable are the significant figures in the child's early life, their awareness will contribute little to influencing that ineffable and crucial milieu of mother and foetus, then mother and infant-foetus/infant with its own genetic disposition, mother with her own disposition cast in a certain phase in her own biographical time. This is to assert that *disposition* is formed early, and by and large in spite of what the mother, or other social agents such as schools, consciously strive to achieve. 'Education' at best allows disposition expression, leads it out; it neither forms nor alters it. This is not to deny that the mother's views of what she is doing, and what she ought to be doing, in raising her child, whether they take the form of common sense or scientific theory, or as is more likely some *mélange* of folk wisdom, ideology and science - that is, in short, her conscious intentions - reflect, both in what they say and in the manner in which they are said, and in the saying applied, that woman's own disposition.

Disposition is the *motif* composed of the major rhythms of being, which are resonated forward, to borrow one of Freud's metaphors, from early childhood across the whole span of an individual's life: the individual wends his way backwards and forwards across these rhythms, projected by them, defined by them, tied by them, however much outside forces may distort their signature tune. Disposition is the thread from which destiny is woven.

Culture does change through time, and so too, therefore, one assumes, must disposition. But what may aptly be termed the Darwinian factor is usually under-estimated, if considered at all, in this discussion. It represents the process operating as the social environment changes whereby new personality types are selected 'naturally' as more fitted to the new conditions: at the same time the types that were the best 'adapted' (successful, productive, content or whatever are the preferred criteria of 'survival') in the old culture find themselves obsolete, struggling against the grain, cast in a time out of joint to them. And we suspect that our history is littered with the unsung corpses of thousands of Christs who came at the wrong time, Churchills for whom the nation was never cast into war unprepared and with low morale, derelict Puritans out of work and far from a pulpit. This is a model of circulating élites, with changes in economic, social and political conditions playing the principal role in writing the entrance qualifications. To introduce the concept 'disposition' is automatically to stress the limited significance of the role that the psychological pliability of specific individuals may play in cultural and social change.

In his study, *Winthrop's Boston*, Darrett Rutman argues that John Winthrop's ideal of founding in Massachusetts a 'city on a hill', a community of men harmoniously linked by covenant, was undermined virtually from the outset by the heterogeneity of those who came to Boston. Boston's population in its first years was peculiarly uniform, made up of men of similar temper and background, in the main radical, devoutly ascetic types; men, that is, of like disposition who in reaction to the growing hostility to Puritanism in England had banded together in common idealism; men who by virtue of zeal and likemindedness would create a more severe climate of piety in the New World than the vast and established heterogeneity of England had tolerated. But in the process they created a community whose prosperity soon attracted men of another kind, drawn by the prospect of material profit. Here is a particular case of a changing socio-economic reality influencing the composition of a community and eventually its hierarchy of privilege, disposition changing in the aggregate, but not in the individual.

If individual disposition is effectively set from infancy, there yet remains the possibility of changes within one family line - that is, phylogenetic changes. Here I again return to Freud, accepting his conviction that phylogeny governs ontogeny, that the sins of the fathers are visited upon the sons. There is no precise formulation to be abstracted here of how much disposition may change from generation to generation. The best we can do is the loose surmise that the thread changes very slowly within the family line.

Is 'disposition' a Puritan notion? Is the remissive justified in his hope that once the sins of the Puritan past are forgiven there will be no more rigidities of character? My answer has been in the negative. The remissive will never achieve his goal of carefree hedonism; he at best learns to play in the interstices between the neuroses his past has lodged, gaining respite now and again. The question then arises, what does it mean to talk of the withering of the remissive's Puritan disposition: what new disposition 'slouches towards Bethlehem to be born'? The rising disposition will likely not appear as clearly to us as Woody Allen's 'something weird and futuristic, with the body of a crab and the head of a social worker'. Apart from Puritan vestiges, it may be depressive, superficially carefree, a Meursault; or then again it may be violently paranoid. But although it will most probably prove elusive to our current categories, and bewilderingly heterogeneous, it will constitute a 'disposition'.

If there is a remissive as there was a Catholic disposition then what is left of the suspicion that there might be something uniquely Puritan about this notion of innate character? The suspicion remains well founded, its issue being at the fulcrum of the remissive revolt against an interdictory culture. Puritanism gave 'disposition' ideological recognition; it built a theology of election that took central account of it. For the early Puritans it was divine parentage that determined character; but this lineage soon translated into 'God has so cast the line of election that for the most part it runs through the loins of Godly parents.' The severity of Puritan morality, the iron band of its commands, represented a strategy for living with disposition, winning a tolerable life from predetermined personality. The descendant of Adam faced the constant threat that he was not chosen, that he was by disposition fallen; he thereby suffered from an irrepressible sense of inadequacy, that his life was invalid, unblessed and tainted; he had, moreover, then to survive the guilt unleashed by unsurety and inadequacy. His response was to subject himself to strict pietistic commands and their translation into hard work, and into vigilant spiritual introspection and exhortation. Such were the consequences of a theology of disposition.

But the fact of 'disposition' - its psychological function, its social and cultural consequences - is universal. What is peculiarly Puritan is recognition of it, and the further consequences of that consciousness. There is no evidence that the Puritan's past is any more binding, in real psychological terms, that any other man's; he does, however, read it as binding and ensures, by cultivating this genre of fatalism as the stem of his morality, that he will not shirk his reading.

Now to return to culture's first function, and its relationship to disposition. Proust writes of a piece of music that he always found compelling, uncannily so; it was as if lodged in its rhythms were some mirroring double of his own, inducing in him an exquisite feeling of harmony. Culture provides a gallery of images, symbols, archetypes, in short, forms, whether expressed as myths, stories, music, philosophy or 'common sense', from which disposition, in browsing, chooses what suits it, what seems to express and give meaning to its own latent form.

The acquiring of culture is, however, for much of the time, a more involved pursuit than simply looking at paintings. Disposition guides men in their choice of the experiments in doing and interacting that constitute the substance of their 'experience'. These experiments themselves contribute images and associations to the individual's living culture, forms by means of which disposition surfaces in the manifold of aspirations, anxieties, gratifications, enthusiasms, antipathies, hurts, that by the fact of having surfaced, with some differentiation, are the more visible and therefore manageable. Such lived forms are then available to be employed, in the guise of memories, when future experiments are being considered. And men do not merely borrow from old paintings, they rework them; and they themselves paint. Culture and experience are mutually conditioning and inseparable, themselves conditioned from one direction, by individual disposition, which selects from them whatever attracts it; they are conditioned from the other direction by their housing society, which provides cultural forms and milieux for experiment, which in their turn are inseparably linked and historically specific.

A series of corollaries, in an enterprise that aspires to return to first principles, now claims enunciation. The expression 'We learn by experience' gains the specific connotation: 'We learn to choose only experiments that will somehow be in key with our disposition.' The hero of Robbe-Grillet's *Les Gommes* turns a routine murder investigation into an autobiographical oedipus fantasy. Or, in the alternative terms of the Abbé Galiani, of which Rieff reminds us, our best hope is that we learn to live with our ailments.

Second corollary: the more disposition has found realization along its key axes, then the more freedom of access the individual may allow himself to the darker axes, those that run to the centre of hurt.

Third corollary, converse of the second: where hurt threatens to overwhelm, disposition will seek security in control by ideology, denying itself expression. Paranoia is disposition so armoured that only at the finger-tip of ideology is the objective world remotely in touch.

Culture's second function is

> to ensure that the moral demands men make upon themselves enable the collectivities to which they belong to function as viable economic, social, and military entities, and to organize those demands into a system of symbols that make men intelligible and, in particular, predictable to each other, thus also rendering the world intelligible.

The two functions necessarily overlap. The cultural forms to which an individual is dispositionally attracted belong to a common culture, and are employed in similar ways for similar reasons by others, who by this very fact become familiar and intelligible. Indeed, one aspect of this second function is to provide compelling common notions of what an individual is and does, how he should conduct himself and moreover how he should cope with vicissitudes and their strain. It hereby serves to support the individual, making his purposes legitimate, reducing his corrosive and anomic sense of isolation; it raises his morale and induces a comforting sense of human solidarity.

Culture in its second function serves additionally to maintain commitments to social goals, to ensure that the milk gets delivered, reinforcing in this case economic and military rather than individual defences.

The objection might be raised that culture has other functions. The one that comes to my mind is aesthetic: it might be argued that culture has the quite independent task of granting an individual the singular pleasure of experiencing beauty. But this case serves, without belittling reduction, as an example of culture in its first function. And, of course, one should add that a shared aesthetic (all aesthetics are shared; the sociological pleonasm is introduced merely for emphasis) satisfies the same individual and communal function as does shared morality, of which it represents, in spite of Mr Oscar Wilde's rhetoric, a sub-species.

Culture can fail, and in different ways. It can fail in its first function, causing those repressions and neuroses that Freud took as the foreground of his interest. We should place in this category the case of a Catholic disposition raised in a severely Puritan society, or the more complicated, and likely, case of some partial discrepancy between disposition and society, for instance, again to summon Freud, of a society whose prohibitions enforce formidable superegos which permit less release from their controls than are tolerable to some individuals. This mode of failure is exhibited when culture largely takes the form of ideology, morally charged meanings that are unresponsive to any of disposition's needs, other than control.

Culture may also fail in its second function. Durkheim's egoistic and anomic suicides provide instances, as does the case of the matured Puritan isolated in a remissive environment, out of work, without partner. As children gaily repeat: 'The polar bear needs snow and ice, to keep his disposition nice.' Culture fails too for that remissive society which becomes so lax that it forgets to defend itself against invading Mongolians.

Finally, there is failure of a type prevalent in Western literature, *tragic* failure, sparked off unquenchably by the clash of the two functions of culture. Emma Bovary, still one of our principal cautionary types, raised on romantic fables, culture to her disposition, has to live as an adult in a bourgeois milieu in a provincial town, a life for which she prepared ideologically, if imperfectly; failure to find a *modus vivendi* destroys her. One might argue that there was too little of the bourgeois in her disposition for her to gain pleasure from making a double life single, from controlling her pleasures, from managing at once public propriety and private illicitness. One might alternatively merely say that social circumstances were against her, or, again, that it was her own hysterical character that conspired her downfall. A doctrinaire Romantic might claim her life a success, an exemplary martyrdom in the cause of passion, and against 'society'.

Her particular case provides access to a more general dimension of cultural conflict, prominent in Northern European civilization in many different forms since the Reformation. The general culture contains two major clusters of symbols, which are transmitted as if they were compatible, indeed integrated, but which polarize once they are thrown into the scrimmage of experience. There is what we may today refer to as the *Romantic* cluster, projecting in the private domain the imagery of the Romance myths of passion, of ecstatic absorption, and of melancholy *Sehnsucht*; projecting in the domain of work the imagery of heroic purpose, of monumental significance and fulfilment and of vocation. The alternative cluster may for convenience here be termed *bourgeois*. It stresses order and security:

marriage cast in the imagery of manners, of moderation and of stability, in short, the imagery of control. In the public domain, the bourgeois cluster stresses career - stable, predictable and contributing to community welfare.

All dispositions have as part of their composition needs for order and security. In the modern West these needs find cultural form in the main in the various dimensions of the bourgeois symbolic. On the other hand, the Romantic cluster has maintained its prominence precisely because disposition has remained very much of its genre. Cultural conflict here emerges in a new light. Culture, operating in its first function, articulates a split that already exists at the level of disposition, making that split disposition manifest in the form of a divided world-view and a divided ethos. The individual's experiments in experience draw him to cultural forms, which are readily available, that show up a contradiction in his disposition. There are, however, also available many modifications of these cultural forms that make some tolerable equilibrium possible, as long as disposition concurs. For instance, Madame Bovary's particular dilemma was averted for many of her contemporaries by their being able to manage a *mariage de convenance*, with a sympathetic husband and enough wealth to be able to enjoy clandestine affairs in the style to which such ladies aspired. Such an efficacious compromise required a modification of both Romantic and bourgeois ideals, a modification only possible if it itself articulated an aspect of disposition.

But what of culture's second function in this case? It operates with elusive complexity. For a start, dominant socio-economic goals have, since the Reformation, been linked in a mutually-reinforcing affinity with bourgeois values and bourgeois customs. Economically-rooted needs have been made intelligible through bourgeois culture. However, at the same time, economically-functional myths, such as that of 'office boy rising to captain of industry', have borrowed from the Romantic ethos. In short, both cultural clusters have been economically relevant.

One vital social purpose is stability, not only for the sake of military and economic viability: individual well-being too is dependent on a more or less predictable environment. Stability depends upon a commonly held system of beliefs that reinforces commitment to ends that are either explicitly collective or accommodated and sanctioned by the collectivity; the behaviour of others who pursue those same ends is thereby rendered intelligible. The Romantic and bourgeois world-views grew up historically together, intimately connected, thesis and antithesis in one psychological dialectic, nurturing and articulating one character disposition. They represented the extremes of wild adventure and relentless control in that disposition and thereby provided a crucial, if often uncomfortable, balance. Together they have contributed to a cultural nexus which has underwritten a type of social stability.

Culture also functions in its second mode to fulfil the individual's longing for community. A bourgeois ethos more obviously contributes to a sense of social solidarity, of individuals and families joined by common manners and common beliefs. But again the Romantic ethos also has a role to play, in providing a means of communication, and therefore of empathy, between individuals with similar dispositions.

Finally, we must recognize that the workings of culture are vastly heterogeneous. Our culture, in particular, is pluralist and many-tiered. Individuals and groups trade in consignments of culture that variously bind them in some directions and distance them in others, that at a more general level covertly integrate them with those from whom they are otherwise distant, and that at a more intimate one covertly separate them off from those with whom they seem friendly. In this market-place new bargains are constantly being struck, some vigorously, some with such casualness that the purchaser seems almost to forget to take away his goods. All of the traders tacitly accept the customs of the market-place, and thereby grant it the status of a collectivity. Market-places remain most obviously nation states, but some more remote supra-national trading posts exist, and there are the many diverse and flourishing bazaars in local areas that maintain the fluency and buoyancy of commerce.

Bourgeois and Romantic cultural clusters are themselves multi-tiered, and their many segments are variously sought at a high price or discounted, according to fashions of disposition and environment. Their homogeneity has had its source in the individual dispositions that needed them, and that employed them in different ways in different spheres of expression. Their significance follows from the prominent role they have played at many levels of cultural experience.

To return now to the problems over assumptions raised in the opening paragraph of this footnote chapter. The psychology I have employed does make central use of the notion 'disposition'; in this it is not restrictively Puritan, although it is indebted to that Puritan contribution to modern cultural science which insists that beyond reason's potentially redeeming powers there stands the impassable fortress of the predestined, the ineluctable, the fated. Similarly, the first function of culture's implication that innate disposition exists is not culturally relative, except in the commonplace sense that our entire scientific orientation is bound up with one historical tradition. Finally, this notion of disposition does not necessarily imply an assumption of the centrality of the individual as a cultural entity, although the notion has come down to us as a derivative of post-Renaissance individualism. Nevertheless, a culture that is deeply conscious of disposition, that has disposition and its consequences as a part of its 'wisdom', is likely to hold the individual in high esteem.

The discussion of *Madame Bovary* provokes a postscript noting some of the limitations of this brief essay. To point to a failure of culture, to describe what has failed to happen, will rarely provide a comprehensive account of a particular case, such as that of Madame Bovary. Moreover, tools have not been forged here for predicting the consequences of such a failure, nor, above all, for judging them. The Romantic reading has as much claim to ethical dignity as any other, even though, as it turns out, it denies one of the analytical claims of this essay, that culture has a second function. My aim here has been to clarify some of my assumptions, and thereby to make certain of my interpretations more visible, their strengths and weaknesses less opaque. These are, nevertheless, the types of assumption and interpretation with which all cultural sociologists must work, one way or another, more or less honestly.

10

On Methods
(Tocqueville, Weber, Freud)

A frontier halts each of the human sciences, far short even of a ridge from which the horizon of total understanding might be glimpsed. The classics come near to this frontier. They are followed by generations who fossick around in their traces, at times raising a better crop from one small piece of land, neglecting others, all the while believing that they are advancing. But the frontier is intractable, in spite of the hopes of the great pioneers that one day some men drawing on their tentative work will progress far beyond and may even reach the ridge. Indeed, after many years during which the land short of the frontier has been overpopulated and overworked, its original fertility long spent, the horde of epigoni begin to withdraw; they now stream towards a newly opened frontier somewhere else, like unlucky diggers hearing the rumour of gold, preferring not to see that Ballarat will be like California, that for them all frontiers will prove to be alike.

Their fathers did not fare better, being the first followers, but not having had to pioneer, to cover vast unknown spaces without an inherited map. They grew dim to where they had come from, and to the purpose of being there at work near one short section of the frontier. They laboured and forgot who or where or why. And it is another mistake to hope that the sum of their labours wins any new territory in the struggle for understanding. For knowing is not the issue of a commune of farmers who share the fruit of their daily toil at sunset, but is rather that of a vast expedition undertaken by one man essentially alone; it is the sum of his discontent at the start, of the first vague plans, of the choosing of direction, the gathering of provisions, the final setting out and then of the long journey in which plans, provisions and ultimately the quality of ambition are tested every day; it is the totality of his enterprise from the cartoon of the grand design down to the multiple of finely-worked strategies developed on the way to cope with hazards of unforeseen detail.

All the pioneers got within reach of the frontier by using the same general strategy, of a bold and simple plan which they stuck to relentlessly, but which they were nevertheless able to adapt and qualify in order to negotiate the storm of daily vicissitudes. That such a plan should take on the diverse burdens of hurdling unexpected obstacles day after day, strapping them on as part of its own unwieldy cargo, and lumber on, even gaining a new balance, and more, finally reach its destination, that is the mark of genius - it is exemplary.

Any excursus in method is a search for faith, and for a rationalization.

11

On Universals:
Weber, Calvin and Oedipus

Whatever their sources, there are universals influencing the motion of human experience and consciousness, although different periods dress them in their own specific cultural forms. I intend here to look at three moments in the history of one dialectical pair of such universals. One universal is 'fate', 'necessity', what is perceived as an incomprehensible, superhuman galaxy of forces controlling human destiny; the other, its complement, is individual freedom, and responsibility, a mode for transcending fate.

In Sophocles' *Oedipus the King*, the dialectic has three elements, the third operating as a synthesis:

1 All is fated, by 'a savage God who burns us' (David Grene's translation). The Chorus sings:

> May destiny ever find me
> pious in word and deed
> prescribed by the laws that live on high:
> laws begotten in the clear air of heaven,
> whose only father is Olympus;
> no mortal nature brought them to birth,
> no forgetfulness shall lull them to sleep;
> for God is great in them and grows not old.

2 To seek after the truth is madness; truth destroys. The implication is that only the ignorant move in the world with a semblance of freedom; they look ahead and forget their past. Oedipus, the naive, so misunderstands his true condition that he is driven to know, particularly about his past. Jocasta laments: 'Best to live lightly, as one can, unthinkingly.' The man 'in whom alone of mankind truth is native', Teiresias the prophet, is blind, and hence past active life, and impotent - Oedipus discounts him as a suspect for Laius' murder because of his blindness. When Oedipus does

finally recognize the truth he destroys his own eyes and casts himself out. Teiresias had warned that human sight sees nothing; it is blind to the logic of fate.

3 Jocasta's hope for living lightly is a delusion. Again Teiresias:

> Of themselves things will come,
> although I hide them
> and breathe no word of them.

Individual freedom, in the sense of self-determination, is a delusion; the ignorant merely believe that they are free. Oedipus leaves Corinth hoping to elude the prophesy that he will kill his father and lie with his mother, but is deluded about the identity of his parents; it is a vicious irony that he kills his father at a crossroads at the foot of Parnassus, the home of the Delphic Oracle. Truth smiles down on the unwitting crime. And later blind Oedipus closes the circle of fate by returning to Cithaeron and the mountainside on which as an infant he was abandoned to die, this time indeed to end his days. The charisma of Sophocles' drama lies in its generative ambivalence, that precisely because there is no freedom, because necessity rules, there is dignity in knowing. Jocasta draws no tears, whereas Oedipus, the naive, for whom the external world had become blighted, attains heroic stature in his singleminded passion to expose the polluting evil, in spite of the madness of that endeavour, which would expose what Teiresias described as the temper lying within him, and destroy him. Oedipus, in his mounting compulsion to know, to know his birth, the truth about his life, the power of oracles, of destiny, makes the prototypal psychoanalytic journey. Sophocles confirms the audience's identification by placing it in Oedipus' own position, tormented by a growing sense of what has really happened and yet hoping for some way out, hoping that there might have been a mistake. Our attention fixes on how Oedipus will bear the truth, what he will do once he recognizes who he is; we ask in short what freedom does he have to counter the dire hand of fate.

It is well recognized that Sophocles' drama presents universal themes, although there may be contention over which precisely are the universals. (I have avoided discussing the universal to which Freud drew our attention, merely for the reason that it is today so much a part of our common wisdom.) I have employed Oedipus here mainly as an introduction to the case by which I am absorbed, that of Calvin. Calvin, who is little read any more, and whose doctrines once known usually elicit bewilderment, was as much as Sophocles a framer of universals.

In Calvin's *Institutes* the fate-freedom dialectic again has three components, which run somewhat parallel to those in *Oedipus the King*.

1 All is predestined, determined by an immeasurable and omnipotent God. 'Nothing happens except what is knowingly and willingly decreed by him' (I:xvi:3).

2 Man has free-will, a conscience, and is responsible. 'Man is not excusable for he received so much that he voluntarily brought about his own destruction' (I:xv:8). It is free-will, actuated and guided by grace, that saves man.

3 Calvin goes to great lengths of sophistry to rationalize the fact that 1 and 2 are in explicit logical contradiction. He, for instance, quotes Bernard with approval:

> Thus the soul, in some strange and evil way, under a certain voluntary and wrongly free necessity is at the same time enslaved and free; enslaved because of necessity; free because of will. And what is at once stranger and more deplorable, it is guilty because it is free, and enslaved because it is guilty, and as a consequence enslaved because it is free. (II:iii:5)

But while man is dependent on saving grace, over which he has no control, there are ways of living in a godly manner:

> (i) Gaining wisdom, which has two parts, knowledge of God and of self, which are mutually dependent. However, Calvin's ambivalence recurs here, as everywhere: we never understand much because 'the fault of dullness is within us'.
> (ii) Looking to his calling, and this primarily, Calvin argues, as a means of self-control: 'Therefore each individual has his own kind of living assigned to him by the Lord as a sort of sentry post so that he may not heedlessly wander about throughout life' (III; x; 6).

That these doctrines are absurdly inconsistent on a rational plane confirms the view that their appeal was psychological, that the logic they articulate belongs to the psyche. This logic is persuasive at a number of different levels. In the first place, all men, except perhaps those who have indomitable faith in their religion, experience their existence - where they come from, where they are going, how they should live - as a process over which they feel themselves to have at best intermittent control. In short, 'fate' rules and is responsible for the good and the bad. This is a universal, although one whose operation will be aggravated or eased by particular social conditions. But men under the rule of fate still suffer from anxiety, as did Oedipus, bound to his past by guilt; they have consciences, and the implication of the continued experience of guilt is that they have erred or sinned; to sin requires free-will. Thus Bernard's 'it is guilty because it is free', indeed his entire dialectic, makes fine psychological sense.

There is a further dimension adding to Calvinism's interpretative cultural force here: to sense the omnipotence of necessity, and still to suffer guilt, ensures that fate will be experienced as a persecuting God, an unjust ruler. A religion that idealizes the persecuting God performs the important cultural function of interpreting and justifying the human plight to humble man. In addition, the combination of necessity and guilt would prove intolerable without some semblance of hope for redemption; therefore this religion becomes even more telling when it holds out qualified possibilities for remission. Vocation has for the Puritan the crucial function of providing a means, alternative to depression or madness, for dealing with the kingdom of a persecuting God.

Calvinism gains power not only from its articulation of fate and the ensuing paradox of guilt, but from a whole series of dualisms. Calvin's almost Tertullian logic holds in effect that

> redemption is available, but man never escapes his guilt;
> assurance is possible, yet man can never be confident; wisdom is
> crucial, but man never understands much; man must work, but
> works are irrelevant; man is responsible for himself, yet God
> determines all.

This is a theology of ambivalence, and here resides its deepest psychological pull. It supplies symbolic form for the ambivalence of instincts that Freud insisted governed human behaviour, an ambivalence ranging from the epic war of eros and aggression to the multiple conflicts of simple wishes. Calvin's theology does this by facilitating the projection of instinctual vicissitudes and their patterns of guilt on to a cosmic moral plane, on to a comprehensive world-view and a commanding ethos. Its very harshness is compelling; severe inner tension may be controlled if there is a strong stoic ethic for it to grasp hold of.

There is a last consideration relevant to Calvinism's psychological plausibility. The dualist universal, which I have discussed in terms of 'instinctual ambivalence', has a complementary opposite: the monist universal establishes the principle that all is ultimately united and harmonious, that the same purpose governs all things, the same truth encompasses all things. Men inform and sustain their dualist reality with hope for a monist utopia. Calvinism also accommodates the monist universal with peculiar success. It does so through the extremity of its doctrine of divine omnipotence, its assertion that a single entity, God, determines all, according to his own single purpose. Man accordingly has one end in life, to attain salvation; all he does and knows has significance only in terms of that end. Calvinism, taken as a whole, provides a symbolic powerfully representing the totality of the dualist-monist dialectic.

I wish finally to look at leading themes in the work of Max Weber from the perspective of the universals that have emerged from Calvin's *Institutes*. It is not surprising that the work of the man who interpreted Calvinism as having played the prominent intellectual role in the development of modern Western society should itself give similar expression to these same universals. For Weber, for whom there was no God, although he did use the term 'gods' in a casual sense to refer to ultimate values, fate had come to take the form of an 'iron cage' of economic determinism, of an institutional order, which, once its embryonic form had been decided upon after the Reformation, had progressively taken over, developing according to *its* own laws. These laws were so complex as to be resistant to human understanding in any substantive sense, the human mind being indeed too 'dull'. Moreover, capitalist development, working through time by its own logic, had increasingly come to distort the purposes of individual men to fit its own goals. Confronted by its iron determinism, the individual was now, by the early twentieth century, powerless.

Yet Weber, like Calvin, could not accept total determinism: he constantly sought through his work an alternative, a way off the rigid path that his scholarship suggested the West was doomed to follow. He discussed whether an 'irrational' charismatic type of authority and leadership might be able to counter bureaucratic rationality; he hoped for a man with such a vocation for politics that he might spring the iron cage open. Here in his meditations on human possibility in the face of a persecuting God, Weber not only retrieved Calvin's own notion of 'calling', but, in his explication of the qualities needed by the man of politics, he singled out precisely Puritan virtues, those of passion, understanding (the product of dedicated, relentless investigation), and responsibility. His work at this point mirrors the theological debates of the early seventeenth century in England, which had taken up Calvin's worry about how the individual might have a role to play in a determined world. Finally, Weber, at the end of his 1918 lecture, *Science as a Vocation*, without supplying any justification, called for men to accept the challenges of the 'demands of the daily'. With this call a distinction is established in his work that exactly parallels Calvin's separating off important, other-worldly questions, which are matters for God alone and beyond human comprehension, from the mundane, this-worldly affairs of men, for which those men are wholly responsible.

There are telling similarities between Calvin and Sophocles. Apart from their common concern with the determinedness of things, there is the fact that Oedipus, in endeavouring to escape from his oracled fate, gambles on the individual having some free will. He who had saved Thebes by outwitting the Sphynx (symbol of the oracular, the supernatural, of determined destiny) sought an individual principle with which, if not to overrule the gods, at least to win some independence from them. Calvin's awkward attempt to combine grace and free will is analogous. But there are differences: fate decrees that Oedipus is doomed. He is heroic in that his fate was grand and in that he tenaciously sought to know it, thus willing on himself its final judgment. For Calvin there can be no understanding for the unchosen, for the doomed; and they are not exemplary. (There might be a point to arguing that in the terms of Greek tragedy Oedipus was one of the 'chosen'.) Here, Weber's vision is closer to that of Sophocles, for the fate he glimpses is a damning one, and the only path really open to him is that of understanding, relentlessly to lay bare the lineaments of disaster, while hoping, futilely, each moment, that there might be a way out.

By now it must be apparent that the particular historical and psychological construct, the 'Puritan', as I have used it, is veined with universals. Puritan culture was a way of addressing through one phase of history the universal problems of spirit and matter, of egoism and community, of control and release, and the universal themes of authority, responsibility and fate. These problems and themes were coloured, as they always are, by the time; so were Puritanism's solutions.

Discussions about universality are old, and have been conducted in many contexts. Indeed, it is almost an article of literacy to have posed the question of what it might mean to claim that Shakespeare is universal, that he transcended his own time. Drawing on the earlier discussion of culture and its functions it is now possible to make a few specific comments. There are universal experiences, whether of biological, psychological or sociological semblances, derivatives of such facts as the following: all men are born of a mother into many years of dependency, all men participate in groups, all men have erotic impulses some of which are bound to be frustrated, all men are spectators at their own physical decay. These experiences gain formative expression through culture; but culture is specific, varying from one society to the next. (Cultural forms themselves may well contain universal elements of their own. For instance, there may be conventions of story-telling or conventions of how a comedy or a tragedy works that are invariant from culture to culture. What is certain is that cultural forms in part obey a logic independent of the individual employing them: he has to fashion his sense within the given laws of, to take one example, his chosen language.) The varieties of cultural form govern the weight accorded to different universals, the balance between them, and the manner in which they vein social life. When men do manage to talk to each other across time or across social boundaries it is because they have managed to read in the cultural forms of each other representations of those universals that have a similar significance to themselves. But the balances are in perpetual motion and myths must be constantly reinterpreted, or lose their cultural relevancy.

12

Motives

I like our time: undistorted by the worry and bustle of war, economic privation or despotism. It has the possibility to be a clear and free time, the light stark, the relief of the human landscape sparse and bold, few nooks for distraction.

Every time provides the material for many stories. I have told one. Better a caricature than a clutter of lines and shades. So said the court jester.

It has been suggested that the whole of world literature is composed of a few simple stories, should we not say universals, which are told and retold in different forms. So too there are a few elemental social philosophies, perspectives for viewing the human condition. Thus it is one of our tasks to remind ourselves, and others, of the old half-forgotten story that seems again to fit us well. We do this by retelling it in more familiar images. So Weber retold seventeenth-century Puritan theology, which had retold Calvin, who had retold Augustine, who had retold Paul and so on.

Carlyle saw his time longing for the antique world of Walter Scott, in which men were men. Western culture, from the Old Testament prophets, is littered with the shrill soundings of those discontented with their present, idealizing some moment from the past. The flight from the present is compounded in the Puritan tradition by a striving for this-worldly perfection: the unredeemably blemished, that which does not bear in it the possibility of fulfilment of purpose, stands as an intolerable insult to man's divine aspirations. Hence the moralist rage against the foibles of daily human reality, the intolerance of the impure. These tentacles of conscience inevitably wrench the lines patterning any work of Puritan culture to match their will. But I hope to have indicated, working comparatively through time, an evolution whose roots are slightly more universal than those of my own prejudices.

There is little strength here for prophecy, either of doom or utopia; nothing sought but the quiet we may find in a starker recognition of where we are. Such is the aloof command of knowledge. Yet we are men, duty bound and driven to take up the surgeon's knife, for our body politic is melancholy. We cannot afford, individually or collectively a knowledge that serves alone as an elegant cloak gracing our walk.

'Those who cannot remember the past are condemned to repeat it.' This noble humanist sentiment is propounded and cherished by those intellectuals condemned to believe that their work has political significance, that they in fact are the true men of action, those who command the first causes in great historical chains. But it is a lie. Whether or not the past is to be repeated depends on the disposition not the self-understanding of the present. Sociologists, for example, know that individuals use groups for the working out of their own unconscious compulsions, yet the groups that sociologists themselves form are no less tossed by the irrational momentum of personal projection. And psychoanalysts sadly discovered that clarity about neurosis does not normally signify that the patient has released himself from that neurosis. If understanding has any link with repetition it is in the sense that a true knowledge of the past may itself be a symptom of that phase of the past now seen clearly being over, at a distance and no longer binding. But a symptom is not a cause.

Of course, this means that knowledge, except the instrumental positivist knowledge of a Machiavelli, is politically irrelevant. But this too is a half-truth. What of the great leader, the Abraham Lincoln, who knows his people - their dispositions, their traditions, what they are capable of and which institutions suit them best - who understands the logic of the present, and succeeds as well as possible in preparing the ship for a benign long-term course?

The tiresome old conflict of is and ought, of description and prescription, of diagnosis and therapy. Why the moralist devil who is not satisfied with my account of how I am sad, and demands that I find myself a cure, and, more, that the account be the cure? Children squeal with delight when the magician pulls the rabbit out of the hat. But we adults know a hoax. And this devil is so unkind to my sadness; he so fears pain himself that he would take any drug to stifle the moment. Kraus: 'A single man can neither help his age nor save it, he can only express its decline.'

'The subjective' is treated by most behavioural scientists as a source of systematic error, while the psychoanalyst treats it as the main source of information, simply because his didactic analysis enabled him to tolerate such subjective information. . . . The analyst does not really interpret the patient's unconscious, but the reverberations of the patient's unconscious in his own, which, fortunately, is much like that of the patient, but more accessible to inspection and rational utilization. . . . Psychoanalysis provides the methodological and epistemological paradigm for the behavioural sciences. (George Devereux)

To deny the fact that everything one does is a personal statement is futile. A quasi-participant in the student movement and its concerns in the late 1960s in Europe, I seem to have felt the need to attempt a last judgment. The revaluation whose expression is this book had something to do with an emerging conviction that two axioms central to the left's case are false. First, it is false that repression rather than anomie is the more corrosive psychological force in contemporary Western society. It is equally false that anomie is the alienation of the rich, repression that of the poor. A corollary is that evil as well as good is innate to the human condition. Another corollary is that freedom and equality are antitheses. Second, it is false that men, and their unconscious wishes that are society, can change either quickly or predictably. Idealists are both cruel and deluded to plan with their ideal in mind, Procrustes who do not take account of men's inviolably different levels of ability, tolerance and desire.

One furiously thinks up alibis at the end of the day to deny, not that one is a criminal, but that one is a simple-minded criminal.

It should be demanded of every sociologist that he comes to know the idealized self-image in terms of which he judges the world; that he assesses what in that image is universal, that is, what represents physical and psychological health; that he assesses what in that image is culturally relative, and when neurotic, weighs up the gains against the costs; that he assesses how all this squares with the social and historical necessity in which he is cast, and if it does not, that he amends his sociology in spite of the compelling image; that he interprets why he should have been driven to impose this self as sociology, rather than in the form of other social activity. When he thereby comes to recognize the moral tone of what he is doing, he may have some right to be taken as an authority on some aspects of his time. It is not that he ought to confess in public, even if he has both the ability and the inclination, but rather that his work gain the tension of having its subjectivity conducted at arms length, where it can, to a modest degree, be grappled with. I cannot claim to have done very much of this, although the command has lurked in the back of my mind as I have proceeded, uneasily. And I do tell myself that I have at least reckoned the costs of high Puritan neurosis against the gains of the culture it fashioned. Only when our inherited assumptions and perspectives have been wrecked, our hopes battered on the reefs of our reality, and we have reduced ourselves to a state of hesitant anxiety about whether we can explain anything, may sociology begin. Our ideals are so absurdly demanding, which means glamorizing.

We walk across open country. There is no semblance of a track ahead, but whenever we look behind we are astonished to find that a serviceable and seemingly much travelled road leads up to precisely the spot we have reached. Moreover, along this road come supplies, manpower and instructions - although it is not clear from whom, or about what. And there come other people, most of them, paradoxically, passers-by. Many stop to chat, providing a welcome distraction from our perplexing endeavour. Other self-appointed pioneers occasionally also come our way, but it has always been the case that we are quickly disappointed, finding that they know no more than we do. Very soon, in fact, one should admit, almost immediately, we take to studying the road behind, and its traffic, hoping to lay bare the clue to where we are going. Yet we remain uneasy on our walk in the lovely country, for we suspect that this is not the way.

Sociology is infatuation for an old, indescribably ugly, and very possessive whore, which is sustained by fuzzing the reality with an endless series of fantasies about her hidden beauty. We sociologists are as eager young men searching to read in the wrinkled face and the worn flesh some great truth about the infinity of human ways that she has experienced. We like her agedness, for in it we read rootedness; and however clearly we come to recognize her true state, that death now is the only consummation that awaits her, we are driven to imagine that one day she will find the elixir of youth and be reborn, bearing in her charge all the positives she had so dearly accumulated, shedding their negatives. So it might be said that we are not yet ripe. If we were able to listen to Oedipus, rather than sitting in stunned elation at his tale, we might come to suspect that death longings were the shadows tracking our every step, death longings in the guise of the pursuit of understanding.

Bibliography

ARENDT, HANNAH, 'Society and Culture', *Daedalus*, vol. 89, no. 2, Spring 1960.

BENDIX, REINHARD, *Work and Authority in Industry*, Wiley, New York, 1956.

BETTELHEIM, BRUNO, 'The Problem of Generations', *Daedalus*, vol. 91, no. 1, Winter 1962.

BETTELHEIM, BRUNO, 'Obsolete Youth', *Encounter*, vol. 33, no. 3, September 1969.

CARROLL, JOHN, *Break-Out from the Crystal Palace*, Routledge & Kegan Paul, London, 1974.

CREWS, FREDERICK C., *The Sins of the Fathers*, Oxford University Press, New York, 1966.

DEVEREUX, GEORGE, *From Anxiety to Method in the Behavioural Sciences*, Mouton, The Hague, 1967.

DODDS, E. R., *The Greeks and the Irrational*, University of California Press, Berkeley, 1964.

DURKHEIM, EMILE, *Suicide*, Routledge & Kegan Paul, London, 1952.

EISENSTADT, S. N. (ed.), *The Protestant Ethic and Modernization*, Basic Books, New York, 1968.

ERIKSON, ERIK H., 'Reflections on the Dissent of Contemporary Youth', *Daedalus*, vol. 99, no. 1, Winter 1970.

ERIKSON, KAI T., *Wayward Puritans*, Wiley, New York, 1966.

FEUER, LEWIS S., *The Conflict of Generations*, Basic Books, New York, 1969.

GALBRAITH, J. K., *The New Industrial State*, Hamilton, London, 1967.

GEERTZ, GLIFFORD, *The Interpretation of Cultures*, Basic Books, New York, 1973.

GRAY, FRANCINE DU PLESSIX, 'Blissing Out in Houston', *New York Review of Books*, vol. 20, no. 20, 13 December 1973.

HENRY, JULES, *Culture against Man*, Random House, New York, 1963.

HILL, C., *Society and Puritanism in Pre-Revolutionary England*, Secker & Warburg, London, 1964.

HILL, C., *Intellectual Origins of the English Revolution*, Oxford University Press, London, 1965.

HILL, C., *Reformation to Industrial Revolution*, Weidenfeld & Nicolson, London, 1967.

HOFSTADTER, RICHARD, *The Paranoid Style in American Politics and Other Essays*, Jonathan Cape, London, 1966.

KENISTON, KENNETH, *Youth and Dissent*, Harcourt, New York, 1971.

KOLAKOWSKI, LESZEK, 'My Correct Views on Everything', *Encounter*, vol. 44, no. 6, June 1975.

MANNHEIM, KARL, *Essays on the Sociology of Culture*, Routledge & Kegan Paul, London, 1956.

MILLER, PERRY, *Errand into the Wilderness*, Harvard University Press, Cambridge, Mass. 1956.

MILLER, PERRY, *The New England Mind, the Seventeenth Century*, Harvard University Press, Cambridge, Mass., 1967.

MONEY-KYRLE, R. E., *Psychoanalysis and Politics*, Duckworth, London, 1951.

MORGAN, EDMUND S., *Visible Saints*, Cornell University Press, Ithaca, 1965.

MORGAN, EDMUND S., *The Puritan Family*, Harper, New York, 1966.

NISBET, ROBERT, *The Twilight of Authority*, Oxford University Press, New York, 1975.

RIEFF, PHILIP, *Freud, The Mind of the Moralist*, Gollancz, London, 1960.

RIEFF, PHILIP, *The Triumph of the Therapeutic: Uses of Faith after Freud*, Harper, New York, 1966.

RIEFF, PHILIP, *Fellow Teachers*, Harper, New York, 1973.

RUTMAN, DARRETT B., *Winthrop's Boston*, University of North Carolina Press, Chapel Hill, 1965.

SCHÜCKING, L. L., *The Puritan Family*, Routledge & Kegan Paul, London, 1969.

SIMMEL, GEORG, 'On the Concept and the Tragedy of Culture', *The Conflict in Modern Culture and Other Essays*, Teachers College Press, New York, 1968.

SLATER, PHILIP E., *The Pursuit of Loneliness*, Beacon, Boston, 1970.

STEINER, GEORGE, *In Bluebeard's Castle*, Faber & Faber, London, 1971.

TOCQUEVILLE, ALEXIS DE, *Democracy in America*, 2 vols, Colonial Press, New York, 1900.

TOFFLER, A., *Future Shock*, Random House, New York, 1970.

WATKINS, OWEN C., *The Puritan Experience*, Routledge & Kegan Paul, London, 1972.

WEBER, MAX, *The Protestant Ethic and the Spirit of Capitalism*, Allen & Unwin, London, 1930.

I am deeply grateful to Sandra Lauderdale for many testing comments, to Lotte Mulligan and to Ronald Bush for scrupulous stylistic criticism.

Index

Bunyan, John 6
Bureaucracy, growth of 30; as paranoid defence 84
Burgess, Anthony 90
Burke, Edmund 89

Cage, John 54; quoted 54
California 38, 123
Calvin, John 15, 132; ambivalence of 128–9; compared with Sophocles 130; compared with Weber 130; contradictory logic of 127–9; English followers of 98–9; fatalism of 98, 127–9, 130; notion of visible Church 98; praise of doubt 97–8, 103; on responsibility 98, 127; on salvation 98, 127, 129, 130; universals in 127–9, 130; on vocation 98, 127, 130; quoted 97, 98, 127; *see also* Calvinism
Calvinism, asceticism 10; doctrine of election 8, 46, 103, 104, 105; doctrine of election revised 98–9, 100–1, 109, 110; theological weakening of 98–9, 100, 104; *see also* Puritan
Cambridge Calvinists 98–9
Camus, Albert 26, 27, 45, 51, 98
Capitalism 10, 28, 30, 31–2, 38, 88, 99; consumption 20, 22, 30, 56; its future 93–4; production 20, 22; viewed as evil 78
Carlyle, Thomas 84, 132; quoted 97
Cartesian Meditations (Husserl) 34
Castaneda, Carlos 91
Catholicism 21, 41, 116, 118
CBS, reporting of fall of Saigon 66
Cézanne, Paul 52, 56
Charisma 30, 31, 39; in Dimmesdale's sermons 108; of *Oedipus the King* 126; and cultural change 62; in teaching 46; Weber's concept of 129; in work 73
Childhood 113–14
Childhood and Society (Erikson) 68
Chopin, Henri 53
Christ, Jesus 70, 114
Christianity 97

Church, its function 97; visible and invisible 98, 103
Churchill, Winston 114
Cithaeron 126
Citizenship 46
City 58–9
Clockwork Orange, The (film) 90
Columbia University 72
Commerce, as metaphor for culture 121
Community 47–8
Conflict of Generations, The (Feuer) 66
Congregationalist, model of Church organization 101
Conservative, response to cultural conflict 18, 86
Conspiracy theories 13–14, 80
Corinth 126
Cotton, John, theology of 99–100, 104, 107
'Counter-culture' 26, 77, 85; its metapolitics 80
Court jester 132
Covenant theology 98–9, 100
Criminal, the 65, 134
Cromwell, Oliver 10, 16
Culture, central question of, in West 99; change 114, model of 85, periods of 60, 88–9; Christians, early 100; conflict within 18, 19; Romantic-Bourgeois example of 119–22; degradation of 56, 81; and disposition 114–15, 116–18; failure of 73, 118–21; its forms 117, 120, 131; Freud's equation with renunciation 64; functions of 23, 113–22; defined 18; heterogeneity of 121; popular 82–3; Puritan 109; relativity of 113, 131; and social stability 120–1; sociology of 88; tragedy of 20; and universals 131

Dadaism 51
Darwinian factor 114–15
Decadence, Spenglerian 93
Decadents, *fin de siècle* 59
De-definition of Art, The (Rosenberg) 55
Delinquent, the 65; and nihilism 90–1

weak 68–72
Fathers and Sons (Turgenev) 68
Fatherless society 90
Feminism 41, 47, 81
Feuer, Lewis, on irrational politics 75;
on student radicalism 66–8, 70–1
Film 58
Film-stars 82–3
Fin de siècle 90
Flaubert, Gustave 23, 53, 55; on 'art for
art's sake' quoted 52; *Madame
Bovary* 119–22
Folk wisdom 114
Ford, Henry 30
Forms, in art 51, 53–6; culture's
116–18; in drama 57; remissive
hostility to 87; their function 48
Fortuna 39
Frankfurt School 35
Freedom, antithesis of equality 134; as
a universal, in Calvin's *Institutes*
127–9, in *Oedipus the King* 125–6,
in Weber's work 129–30
French Revolution 70
Freud, Sigmund 118, 119, 126; on
aggression 86; on ambivalence 63;
on child development 17, 113, 114;
cognitive aim of 24–5; on cultural
conflict 118–19; as exemplar sociologist 123–4; as father of the
remissive 16, 17, 34; his followers
25–6; on homosexuality and
paranoia 69; on instinctual renunciation 10, 17, 89; on narcissism 61; on
the past 115, quoted 17; on play 23;
on punishment 102; as Puritan 17,
91; on repressed destructiveness 85;
as subjectivist 33, 51; technique of
21; therapeutic aim of 21, 24, 25

Galahad 72
Galbraith, J. K. 30
Galiani, Abbé 117
Genesis myth 93
Genou de Claire, Le (film) 91
German, language 81; youth 68
Ginsberg, Allen, quoted 55
Goethe, J. W. von 64, quoted 61–2, 94

Goffman, Erving 57
Gommes, Les (Robbe-Grillet) 117
Goodman, Paul 62
Gourmets 43
Graduate, The (film) 62
Greek fatalism 23, 125–6
Greening of America, The (Reich) 27
Guilt, of ambivalent son 102, 103, 104;
and Calvinism 128; Hawthorne
quoted on 106–7; and Hester Prynne
105–7, 109–10; as passion 109–10;
Puritan sublimation of 86
Guru Maharaj Ji 77

Handicapped, the 65
Harvard Law School 72
Haute Couture 22
Hawthorne, Nathaniel 106, 107, 109,
110, 111; on ambivalence quoted
105, 109–10; on guilt 6; quoted
106–7; quoted 106, 108
Hegel, G. W. F. 33
Heidegger, Martin 33, 34, 91; on
beauty 56; and nihilism 34–5
Heine, Heinrich 81
Hell's Angels (motorcycle gang) 82
Hesse, Hermann 76
Hill, Christopher 10
Hitler, Adolf 68, 90
Hobbes, Thomas 32, 89
Ho Chi Minh 65
L'Homme naturel 32
Homo sapiens 93
Homosexuality 69
Household neurosis 86–7
Hume, David 33, 80, 89
Husserl, Edmund 33, 34, 35, quoted 34
Hutchinson, Anne 100
Huysmans, J.-K. 59

Idealism, as cruel 134; and paranoia
80–1
Ideology, and disposition 117, 119; end
of 35–6; as paranoid defence 83–4;
see also Remissive
Iliad, The (Homer) 23
Individual, *see* Puritan
Individualism 122

personal and political 65; *see also* Puritan

Moreau, Frédéric (character in Flaubert's *L'Education sentimentale*) 23

Morgan, Edmund S. 110

Mosca, Gaetano 44

Moses 16, 71

Mothers, dominant 69; as failures 72; nihilism of 72; and infants 114

Music, contemporary 54; pop 58; Proust's archetype from 116–17; remissive 77

Music for Piano (Cage) 54

Napoleonic megalomania 66

'Narcissism of minor differences' 61–2

Narragansett Bay 100

Nature, Man's relation to 93; and nurture 113; Puritan attitude to 78

Nazi ideology 15

Nechaev, Sergei 90

New England settlers 99–104

Newport, Rhode Island 100

Newtonian mechanics 54

Nietzsche, Friedrich 25, 74; on asceticism 10; on German philosophy 33; on moralism 85; on nihilism 36, 89, 90; on psychological man 34; as Puritan 17, quoted 24; and remissive 17; as subjectivist 33–4, 35, 51

Nihilism 61, 87, 90, 103; consequence of weak fathers 90; Dostoevsky and Nietzsche's prophecy 89; epistemological 33, 34–5, 36, 38; parental 71, 72; and student radicalism 67; threat of, and positivism 83

Nihilist-delinquent 90, 92

Nihilist-depressive 90, 93

Nouveau roman 52

'Obsolete Youth' (Bettelheim) 72–3

Occam's razor 83

Odysseus 70

Oedipal, fantasy 117; resentment 66

Oedipus the King (Sophocles) 23, 125–6, 130

Old Testament prophets 132

Olympus 125

Ontogeny 115

Opera 58

Ophelia 91

Orpheus 64

Painting 51, 52, 53, 55–6, 117

Paper Chase, The (film) 72

Paranoid: and adolescence 74; and bureaucracy 84; character, defined 12–15; chronic 79; community 77; and cultural change 60–87; idealization of delinquency 91; and disaster films 85; and disposition 117–18; and environmentalism 78–80; and forms 87; functional to radical politics 60; link with homosexuality 69; and idealism 80–1; and mass media 81–3; middle-class 76; as nihilist-delinquent 90; as parricidal 67; and politics 13–15, 76; and positivism 83–4; psychotic 12, 61; and remissive 85–7; and responsibility 13; and social paralysis 79; and the student movement 66–75; vicious circle of 86; and Victorian moralism 84–5; and Vietnam War 65–6

Parents 71

Pareto, Vilfredo 15

Parnassus 126

Parricide 67, 102–4

Passion 23–5; and Hester Prynne 107; Romantic 119

Pathos, compared with ethos 7–8

Paul, Saint 70, 97, 132

Perkins, William 97, 98

Persecuting God 78

Perutz, K. 49

Phèdre (Racine) 23

Phenomenology 26, 34

Phylogeny 115

Physics 54

Pietà (Michaelangelo) 92

Pilgrim Fathers 101

Pirenne, Henri 89

Plato, on weak fathers 37; on magic

and reason 48

Play 22–3; 38, 39, 64, 93

Pleasure 24; contrast to passion 24–5

Politicians, loss of privacy 82–3

Politics, confusion of good and evil in 75; disallows private life 82–3; independence from public opinion 82; irrational 75, 81; Puritan 15, 75–6

Pollock, Jackson 52

Poor, the 65, 67

Popper, Karl 13

Portsmouth, Rhode Island 100

Positivism 33, 133; in administration 35, 36; Kant against 33; Nietzsche and 34; as paranoid 83–4; and Puritan 35; importance for remissive 93

Possessed, The (Dostoevsky) 68

Presbyterians 98, 101

Press, the, distorts reality 81–2; as exploiter of paranoia 81–2; serious press, as corrupt 82

Preston, John 98

Prison-hospital 90–1, 92

Prisons 63

Privacy 82

Procrustes 134

Prodigal Son 102

Protestantism 99

Proust, Marcel 51, 116

Prynne, Hester (character in Hawthorne's *The Scarlet Letter*) 23, 105–12

Psychiatrists 62, 76

Psychoanalysis 17, 24–5, 91, 133; on depression 86; exemplary method of 134; fusion with existentialism 26; and honesty 21; new remissive type of 21; *see also* Freud

Psychotic model of virtue 62–3

Puritan (Puritanism): asceticism 109, 110; authority 5, 8, 10, 29–30; 103; failure of 61, *see also* Authority; and Catholicism 7–8, 21–2; character, analytical significance of 10–11, attitude to failure 8, contradiction within 8–9, defined 3–5,

exemplified in *The Scarlet Letter* 105–12, intensity 8, *see also* Disposition; community 4, 7, 8, 31, 99–101, 111; election, doctrine of 3–4, 7, 8, 10, 105, 116, revision of 98–104, 108–9, two doctrines of 105, 109, 111; excellence 5, 21–2; family (marriage) 5, 6, 49, 109; fatalist harshness 97–8, 107–9, 122, 128–9; friendship (intimacy) 6, 42, 109; honesty 107, lack of 108–9; inflexible 101, 115; intellect 7, 9, 22; inwardness 4, 106; knowledge 33, 35; moralism 17, 18, 77, 85, 116, 132; nature, attitude to 78; passion 23–4, 25, Arthur Dimmesdale's 109, Hester Prynne's 107, 109, 111; patriarchal 32–3, 41; play 22–3; and pleasure 6, 25; politics 15, 75–6, 130; private and public 6, 7, 112; purity 6, 7, 8, 109, 132; repentance 4, 8, 106, 107, 109; in remissive environment 45, 63, 114, 119; responsibility 7, 8, 10, 18, 112; and salvation 3–6, 8, 10, 22, 23, 75, 108, 110, 111; and science 10; on sensuality 6, 7, 41, 109–10; seventeenth-century 3–11, 17, 42, 49, 99–104, 111; transition to paranoid, and students 68–74; and universals 130–1; vocation 4–5, 7, 8, 9, 20, 23–4, 39, 58, 86, 109, 110, 128, Arthur Dimmesdale's 108–9, 111, 112, Hester Prynne's as exemplar 105–6, 111; work, drive, withering of 86–7, *see also* Puritan vocation

Puritan-remissive 19, 49, 91, 92

Quantum mechanics 54

Racial discrimination 22

Radical politics, and paranoia 60, 77–8, 79–80, 81; *see also* Student

Radio-activity 93

Randomness 23; in art 54

Raphael 52

Realism 14

146

Index

Realpolitik 66
Reductionism 113
Reformation, the 88, 120, 129
Reich, Charles 27
Reich, Wilhelm 21
Relativism, as amoral 38; on paranoia
14; and quantum mechanics 54
Religious cults, modern 17, 77–8
Remissive: and the aged 50–1; as
amoralist 17–18, 57; and art 51–8; as
Catholic 21; defined 16–28, 90; and
delinquency 90–1; as depressive 16,
59, 86; economic causes of 20–1,
30–2, 88; and education 45–9; and
environmentalism 79; and the erotic
41–3; hedonist ideology 16, 18, 19,
20, 26–7, 41–2, 46–7, 48, 77, 80,
85, 86, 93; hedonist man 90, 92–4;
historical origins 88–9; hostility to
forms 87; knowledge, attitude to
22–3, 35–6, 50; and music 54; its
norms 18, 77; and paranoid 85–7;
play and work, attitude to 39;
pleasure 25, 30, 45; politics 15; as
post-psychological 26; problem with
repression 86; producing resentment
93–4; society, its viability 89–94;
and theatre 56–8; therapy 92; and
the university 36–7, 80; utilitarian
20
Renaissance 3, 10
Resentment 93–4
Revolutionary ideal, Nechaev 90
Riders in the Chariot (White) 91
Rieff, Philip, on culture 18; on
'psychological man' 26, 117; on
therapeutic 16, 17, 30; quoted
16–17, 20
Rilke, Rainer Maria 64
Robbe-Grillet, Alain 91, 92, 117
Rockefeller, Nelson 82
Rohmer, Eric 91
Roi soleil, le 78
Romantic culture 119–22
Romanticism, and art 38; concern with
self 51; decadent 59; its fables 119;
individualism of 63, 65, 111; omni-
potence myth 70; its passion 40, 81,

119; contribution to remissive 89;
Rousseauist 40, 71
Rosenberg, Harold, quoted 55
Roth, Philip 69
Rothko, Mark 55
Rousseauist, noble savage 64; optimism
21; Romantic 40
Russia 68, 75, 90
Rutman, Darrett B. 100, 110, 115

Saigon, fall of 66
Sainthood, visible 101, 102, 110
Salem 101
Samson 9
Sartre, J.-P. quoted 49
Satan 97, 103
Scarlet Letter, The (Hawthorne) 6,
105–12
Schiller, Friedrich 64
Schizophrenia 62–3, 91
Science 10, 76, 93, 114
'Science as a Vocation' (Weber) 130
Scott, Walter 97, 132
Self-realization 44–7
Senate, U.S. 82
Shame 22, 105
Shepard, Thomas 101; quoted 100
Sibbes, Richard 98
Simmel, Georg, on culture 18, 20, 42,
113
Sisyphus 98
Socialism 14–15
Social worker 115
Sociology, of Calvinism 97–104;
chiliastic 62; of culture 88, 122; and
death 136; of deviance, as paranoid
64–5; dramaturgical 57; its
exemplars 123–4; key problems of
99; current home of relativists 38;
as Romantic 135–6; self-knowledge
as ideal 134–5; lack of self-
understanding of 133; of work 86
Sophocles 125–6, 127; compared with
Calvin 130; quoted 125, 126
Sorbonne 68
Souffle au coeur, le (film) 91
Spenglerian decadence 93
Sphynx 130